FIVE GENERATIONS OF
HEDSTROMS

AN AMERICAN BRANCH OF A SWEDISH FAMILY

Mitchell W. Hedstrom

FIVE GENERATIONS OF HEDSTROMS
AN AMERICAN BRANCH OF A SWEDISH FAMILY

iUniverse books may be ordered through booksellers or by contacting:

iUniverse
1663 Liberty Drive
Bloomington, IN 47403
www.iuniverse.com
1-800-Authors (1-800-288-4677)

ISBN: 978-1-5320-9819-2 (sc)
ISBN: 978-1-5320-9820-8 (e)

Library of Congress Control Number: 2020905383

Print information available on the last page.

iUniverse rev. date: 03/20/2020

To Dad and Mom

We're all immortal, as long as our stories are told.
—Elizabeth Hunter (1834–)

Contents

Author's Note Regarding Names   xi
Introduction   xiii

CHAPTER 1   Erik Jonsson Hedstrom   1
CHAPTER 2   Eric Leonard Hedstrom   31
CHAPTER 3   Arthur Eric Hedstrom   47
CHAPTER 4   Eric Leonard Hedstrom Sr.   65
CHAPTER 5   Eric Leonard Hedstrom Jr.   91

Epilogue   113
Acknowledgments   115
Select Bibliography   119
Notes   125

Author's Note Regarding Names

Each of the five individuals who are featured in this book have the names that they were born with at the beginning of each chapter and also nicknames that family members and friends used when they referred to them in parenthesis. In this book, each of these individuals are referred to by their nicknames:

- *Erik Jonsson Hedstrom (Erik).* Although there are some sources that refer to Erik as being spelled Eric, we now know from two sources that the correct spelling of his name is Erik: his birth records in Umea, Sweden,[1] and the letter that he wrote to his brother, Pehr, that was published in the Swedish *Aftonbladet* newspaper, signed "Erik Hedstrom."[2] Erik's wife, Christina Charlotta Fritz Hedstrom, was referred to as "Charlotte" in the 1850 Census and in her obituary.

- *Eric Leonard Hedstrom (Leonard).* He was referred to as "Leonard" in the 1860 US Census.

- *Arthur Eric Hedstrom (Arthur).* He was generally referred to as "Arthur."

- *Eric Leonard Hedstrom II (Eric Sr.).* Eric Sr.'s grandfather (Eric Leonard Hedstrom) had died by the time he was born, so after his son (Eric Leonard Hedstrom Jr.) was born, he became known as "Eric Sr."

- *Eric Leonard Hedstrom III (Eric Jr.).* He legally changed his name to Eric Leonard Hedstrom Jr. because he said that the Roman numerals at the end of his name sounded too much like the kings of England. In his later years, after his father passed away, he informally dropped the "Jr." and referred to himself as Eric Leonard Hedstrom.

Introduction

This book is the story of five generations in one family—all going back along the male or paternal line, starting with the author's father.

The story of this particular Hedstrom family begins with a man who was a soldier in the Swedish Army, named Eric Stolterman (1733–1813), and his wife, Maglena Hansdotter (1738–1795). Together, they had three children: a girl who "died young" and two boys, Eric and Jonas. Both of these boys eventually decided to adopt the surname of Hedstrom. In fact, both of them were listed as being parish tailors in the small village of Roback, about two miles south of the city of Umea in the north of Sweden. Jonas, the younger of these two boys, was the father of Eric Jonsson Hedstrom (1803–1890), the man who is the subject of our first biographical sketch.

Jonas Hedstrom only lived to be thirty-four years old, as he died of a disease that swept across the country. However, during that relatively short life span, he was married to Maglena Pehrsdotter in 1798, and together they had five children.[1]

In Sweden, there are quite a few families with the surname of Hedstrom. The name is locational in origin. They have taken their names at separate times from various places beginning with "Hed," which is the Swedish word for *heath*. "Strom" is Swedish for *stream*. A heath with a stream running through it was descriptive of the farm in Roback.[2] In 1971, there were more than three hundred Hedstroms listed in the Stockholm telephone directory, so it is a relatively common surname in Sweden.[3]

Chapter One

ERIK J. HEDSTROM
(1803–1890)

Deep within us all is a nostalgia for the
lost community of our ancestors.

GILBERT TRIGANO (1920–2001)

Erik Jonsson Hedstrom
("Erik")

A t seven o'clock on Sunday morning, April 23, 1843,
the sails were hoisted, and the sailing ship *Hindoo*
pulled away from the dock in Old Stockholm,
bound for America. Among its passengers were Erik and
Charlotte Hedstrom and their seven-year-old son, Leonard.
At that time, Erik wrote the following in his diary:

> As the breeze filled the sails, we viewed for
> the last time the place where both my wife
> and I had spent a full 20 years. This place
> had also been the spiritual birthplace to
> both of us. We had so many good friends
> there, many of whom now stood on the
> shore waiving with their handkerchiefs to
> bid us their farewell. It was to us a solemn
> and memorable day.[1]

In order to take advantage of the wind, Captain Granberg—who Erik referred to as "a resolute and experienced man as far as the sea is concerned"—had decided to take the route north of the British Isles. The weather during the forty-four-day crossing to New York City was stormy, rainy, misty, and cold. The passengers were able to keep dry on deck for only a few days. They apparently experienced some seasickness and bitter cold off the coast of Newfoundland.

At noon on Monday, June 5, the ship sailed into New York Harbor. A few Swedes were there to greet the passengers. During their four-day stay there, they were able to sleep on the ship while exploring Battery Park at the southern tip of Manhattan. Erik and his family then traveled up the Hudson River on a fleet of ten barges to Albany, New York, where they took the six-day trip across the Erie Canal. There were about twenty-two passengers on the canal boat that was drawn by three great, strong horses who plodded along the canal path. In Buffalo, they boarded the steamship *Klinten*, which Erik described as "enormous," to cross the Great Lakes. Finally, they arrived at their destination, the town of Southport, on June 26. Not far from there, Erik purchased forty acres of land, for $1.50 per acre, and a pair of oxen. He then began to build a house.

Roback, Sweden

Erik was born on April 2, 1803, in Roback, Sweden, a little village a few miles south of Umea in northern Sweden. He was the second of five children of Jonas and Maglena

Hedstrom. Jonas had been a parish tailor in Roback. The parents of both Jonas and Maglena had also lived in Roback.[2]

For Erik's parents, there were two very dramatic events that took place in 1809. First, Russian troops occupied Umea for seven days in late May of that year and then again from June 1 until August 23. Second, Jonas—Erik's father—died of a "fever" at the age of thirty-six in April 1809, leaving his thirty-five-year-old wife, Maglena, to provide for Erik and his four siblings (all between ages of one and seven).[3]

Erik wrote the following:

> I remember it well—it was shortly after my father's death—a beautiful morning in the summer. The sun shown so brilliantly and birds sung so beautifully in the trees. Mother was busily sewing and we were chatting and playing. All was at peace in our country home. All at once, we were roused by a cry from our mother saying, "what is that?" as she looked out the window. We all rushed to the window and what a sight—the Russian Cossacks were flanking the fields and their swords were drawn and glistened from the reflection of the sun. We were all in consternation. We ran out and beheld as the Swedish artillery came from another side where they placed themselves not far from our house. Mother, in the greatest rush, packed together some bedclothes and threw them into a wheelbarrow and placed her infant child and another little one on

top of it. I took hold of her skirt and so did the rest and we all went to the river [called the "Ume Alv"] that was nearby, a quarter of a mile in the distance. There she placed all in an area while she ran back for some more. This she did two or three times. Finally, she set off to a place some miles away where some of her friends were.

After a couple of months, we returned to the house that was much damaged. Mother wept so we all wept. It was a hard time. The Lord had visited us with a severe punishment—with war, disease and famine. We had to live for many months on bread made from pine and birch bark mixed with a little barley meal and salt herring.

My mother endeavored to raise us up religiously as well as she understood it. And the Lord blessed her in her endeavors. She often read sermons to us, and prayers out of the prayer book but nothing made such an impression on me as the story of the teachings of Christ; the expression of the love and suffering of Christ. It was through his mercy that I found peace.

My mother, whose heart yearned for me and for my welfare, wished me to learn a trade. But, there was no chance for me in my native place, so mother wrote to a cousin who was then living in Stockholm. She asked him to be so kind and find a place for me there, that I might learn a trade. He answered that I could come and that he had a place for me with a shoemaker.

In May 1817 [Erik was age 14], I said goodbye to my mother who said weeping, "Perhaps I shall never see my son anymore." My relations with my native place [Umea area] were very numerous.

My parents were peasants and very industrious. They had started poor but accumulated some property. I lost my father to a disease that had swept through the country. He was taken with it and he died. My mother was left a widow to care for her five children. It was a turbulent time for her. I did not understand it then but afterward it has come into my mind more vividly—her almost indefatigable exertions and labors to provide for her little ones.[4]

Fortunately, we now know the exact location of Jonas and Maglena's farmhouse and of the twelve parcels of land that they owned. The location was, as Erik described above, in the small village of Roback, just across the river Ume Alve from the city of Umea, about one quarter of a mile from the river.[5]

Somehow through all of the difficulties of the Russian invasion and her husband passing away, Erik's mother,

Maglena managed to survive along with four of her five children. Her daughter Catharina, the third of five by age, had died in March 1810 at the age of five. Also, by 1809, both of Maglena's parents had died.[6]

As Erik's mother kissed him a sad goodbye, and with a knapsack packed with meager food and no doubt the clothes on his back his sole possession, Erik started off on the approximately four-hundred-mile trip to Stockholm, where he finally arrived about two months later "on a lumber ship."

The Setting

During most of the period from 1803 until 1815, Europe was in the throes of the Napoleonic Wars. Sweden was affected by these wars, as it had allied itself with Great Britain against the French Empire and its allies, including Russia. As a result of the Treaties of Tilset in 1807, Napoleon formalized his control over Central Europe while becoming allied with Russia and a truncated Prussia against Great Britain and Sweden. These treaties were partly responsible for starting two wars—the Anglo-Russian War between Great Britain and Russia and the Finnish War between Sweden and Russia.

The Finnish War didn't go well for Sweden.[8] Prior to the war, Finland had been part of Sweden for about seven hundred years. By November 1808, Russia had overrun all of Finland. In the spring of 1809, as Russian troops marched across the frozen Gulf of Bothnia (between Finland and Sweden) and entered Umea on March 24, the king of Sweden was deposed for having lost Finland. The British Royal Navy came to Sweden's defense in the summer of

1809, and the new Swedish King asked Russia for a truce—
which was agreed. Russia and Sweden signed the Treaty
of Fredrikshamn in September 1809 that led Finland to
become an autonomous part of Russia. By 1815, Napoleon
had been defeated in the Battle of Waterloo.

There were several other wars between Sweden and
Russia in the eighteenth century. In addition, Norway
joined with Sweden in a union that lasted from 1814 until
its peaceful dissolution in 1905, with the king of Sweden
also being the king of Norway.[9]

Sadly, there were also several major famines and
epidemics that affected Scandinavia in the nineteenth
century. Between 1866 and 1868, approximately 8.5 percent
of Finland's population died of hunger. Then, from 1867 to
1869, Sweden lost many people to a famine and plague.[10]
Penicillin was not discovered until 1928.[11]

Life in the north of Sweden is also a bit unusual in terms
of sunlight. For example, during the month of January, it
is dark all day and all night, except for about two hours of
sunlight in the afternoon. During the summer solstice in
June, there is sunlight for almost twenty-four hours a day.[12]

Old Stockholm, Sweden

Erik lived in Old Stockholm for most of the twenty-five
years from August 1817 until he left for America in April
1843. He started off as an apprentice to a shoemaker named
Lundstrom. Then he became a journeyman in 1822. The
1825 Census showed Erik living in Old Stockholm with
another shoemaker, his wife, three children, two apprentices,
a nurse, and a maid.[13]

Erik wrote the following:

> In 1826 [when he was age twenty-three], I
> had worked as a journeyman for four years
> in Stockholm and thought to go out on
> my own and be my own boss. But things
> did not go as I wished. My mind was soon
> made up that I should travel to some distant
> port. I first made a journey to the "north
> land" to visit my mother and relations. It
> was now nine years since I had seen her—
> although my oldest sister [Anna Maglena]
> and my younger brother [Pehr] had in the
> meantime come to Stockholm. My mother
> rejoiced much to see me. At first, she did
> not know me as I had changed so.[14]

After her first husband died, Erik's mother, Maglena,
married again twice. Her second husband, whom she
married in 1812, was a widower named Israel Osterstrom, a
tailor and fisherman. He died of a fever at age fifty-three in
1816. Maglena's third husband, who she married in 1820,
was named Johan Johansson Boberg. He died in 1929, so
a few years later, in 1833, Maglena decided to move to
Stockholm where she could be with her daughter, Ana
Maglena, and her sons, Erik and Pehr.[15]

Erik continued in his diary:

> From Stockholm, I started on foot
> towards Denmark with my bundle on my
> back. Then, in April 1826, I arrived in
> Copenhagen. I had no friends there, but as

> I used to belong to a Society of Moravians
> in Stockholm, I looked them up and got
> acquainted with some—which was very
> good for me. By doing so, I was led to a
> better society and kept away from many
> temptations.

> In Copenhagen, I worked for 14 or 15 weeks.
> Then I left and travelled to the Moravian
> village of Christianfeld in Denmark. Here
> I decided to stop. I sought and obtained
> a citation and stayed for three-and-a-half
> years.[16]

Erik obtained a certificate from the parish of Tyrsterup, a town in Denmark that is about 150 miles west of Copenhagen and less than one mile south of Christianfeld. Before 1919, this area was part of Germany. Apparently, Erik worked as a shoemaker in Christianfeld and attended church in Tyrsterup. Christianfeld has recently been described as "a charming place. Time seems to have stood still for 200 years; nothing has been changed and from now on protected as a monument of old architecture."

The village of Tyrsterup was founded by one of the oldest Protestant denominations, called the Moravian Brethren. Erik must have been greatly influenced by this group in religious matters. That may explain why he later spoke critically of the Swedish clergy.[17]

Erik wrote the following:

> For some time, I thought to stay in the
> Moravians Church for good. But my spirit

became restless and wished to come out and see the world more. Finally, I left but not without some reflections. Again I set out on foot and walked through Holstein and into Hamburg by the Elbe. Here I stayed for about six-months. I liked it well there in Hamburg. I got first knowledge of a republican government. That was the reason why I liked it.

From there, I again started on my pedestrian journey to Lybeck and Berlin from where I visited Potsdam [about twenty-two miles Southwest of Berlin]. In these two places— Berlin and Potsdam—I had the chance to visit and see almost all the remarkable things that were to be seen, and military things. But with all of this, I did not like it there. It was despotism and that I hated. Wherever I turned myself, I met or saw soldiers or police. While I was hard at work in Berlin, I got it in my head to visit my native country again. I packed my bundle and started for Rostock [on the Northern coast of Germany], a seaport from where I went on a sailing vessel to Denmark. Then from there, to Helsingborg in Sweden where I stopped to work for some weeks to replenish my purse. Then I again started for Stockholm where I arrived in August 1831 [then age twenty-eight].

> After I had labored for a year for another
> boss, I started to work for myself. For this, I
> had to borrow money. The first years, it was
> very hard to be able to make ends meet.[18]

From Erik's comments above, we see that politics were a consideration in his decision to emigrate—preferring a republican form of government to a monarchy. We also see that religious convictions were also part of the decision, as he tells us that he "used to belong to a Society of Moravians in Stockholm,"[19] and we know that Swedish citizens at that time were not allowed to belong to any religion other than the Swedish Lutheran Church.

Taxes were apparently another consideration, as Erik later said of his life in the US, "all my work is for my own benefit and not, as before, for rent and taxes." Finally, he described America as being a place where "everyone does as he sees fit, without criticism. No one is ashamed to do any kind of work at all."

In 1833, Erik started his own business, and by the age of thirty, he became a master shoemaker and member of the Shoemakers Company.[20]

On September 25, 1834, he was married to Christina Charlotta Fritz ("Charlotte") in the Storkyrkan Church in Old Stockholm.[21] Erik and Charlotte had apparently met each other in Denmark. At the time of their wedding, Erik was thirty-one, and Charlotte was twenty-eight.

Charlotte was born on February 28, 1806, in Vasteras, Sweden, about sixty-five miles west of Stockholm.[22] Her father was also a shoemaker, like Erik. All of her grandparents had also lived in Vasteras. Erik wrote many years later of his wife, "Our marriage has been a blessed one. My wife has been to me true and faithful, a pious and devoted woman."[23]

Erik and Charlotte had a son they named Eric Leonard Hedstrom ("Leonard"), born on August 21, 1835, while they were living at Baggensgaten 21 in the Block Perseus in Old Stockholm—a building that still stands today.[24] It turns out that this was their only child. Before leaving for America, Erik and Charlotte had read several of the America Letters in the Swedish newspaper, *Aftonbladet*, describing the immigration to the US by other Swedes.

Erik wrote the following:

> In 1842, one of our friends who was pretty well informed about America—especially the states of North America—started to talk to us about it—and that he wished to go there and asked if we would want to go with them. At this, we only talked and considered it as a wild and adventurous folly. But he was earnest and gave us pamphlets with descriptions of several states—their climate and fertility. We read and talked about it and our friend spared no pain in encouraging us to go. Our business was such that neither of us could go very soon so we agreed to prepare for a whole year. But the nearer it came towards the time of our departure, the more uncertain it became—but then we concluded to go anyhow. However much we would like to have them with us, we were still in hope

that he would be able to prevail upon his wife. But she said that if he wanted to go, he could but she would not go and neither would any of their children.[25]

Swedish Emigration to America

The Great Migration from Sweden to America took place between 1840 and 1940. During that time, approximately 1.2 million Swedes, out of a population of about six million, emigrated—or one out of every five Swedes.[26]

There were some liberal voices that said this emigration was somehow symptomatic of serious problems at home.[27] These people had been inspired by the French Revolution in 1789 and the principles of the Enlightenment—self-determination, the leveling of class distinctions, popular sovereignty, and constitutionally guaranteed rights of citizens. For them, America may have represented the "last best hope for humanity" or "the promised land." In their minds, America ceased to become a place and gradually became an ideal.[28]

However, there were also conservative voices in Sweden that said the departing Swedes were only chasing a soulless materialism, that the emigrants were irresponsible and unpatriotic dreamers who were abandoning their homeland.

Several factors explain the huge numbers. There was growing dissatisfaction of the Lutheran Church at home, which had been the state religion in Sweden since 1593. In the nineteenth century, various royal decrees and acts of parliament forbade Swedes from practicing any religion other than the mandatory Lutheran Sunday mass. Without the presence of a Lutheran clergyman, public gatherings were forbidden. It remained illegal for Swedes to convert to another religion until 1860. By comparison, America's promise of religious freedom was a powerful inspiration for many Europeans.[29]

In the early part of the nineteenth century, there was compulsory military training in Sweden at the age of twenty. There was also the Swedish practice of primogeniture, where family farms had traditionally been left to the oldest son, leaving the younger sons and the daughters feeling left out. Finally, there was the issue of social inequality at home, with the royals and the common folk, as opposed to the promise of social mobility and egalitarianism in America.[30]

Swedish emigration had really started in 1638 when a group of fifty Swedes emigrated and settled near the Delaware River in America, calling their new home New Sweden. This settlement grew to about five hundred people before it was lost to the Dutch in 1655. This early settlement created an interest in the US among Swedes.[31]

Four events occurred around 1840 that probably triggered the Great Migration. First, in May 1840, there was an ordinance in Sweden that removed the requirement that any emigrant must obtain the king's permission before embarking on any foreign travel.[32] Second, in America, an act of Congress in 1812 created the General Land Office to handle the sale of land that had been ceded to the US by various Indian treaties.[33]

Another act of Congress in 1832 permitted cash sales of this land in forty-acre lots at a minimum price of $1.25 per acre. To prevent speculation, the purchaser had to intend to use the land for cultivation, and affidavits swearing to this intent were required. (The subsequent Preemption Act of 1841 and the Homestead Act of 1862 also facilitated the westward expansion of the US through land sales to individuals who were living on the land.)

There was a belief at the time—known as Manifest Destiny—that America was destined to expand across the continent to the Pacific Ocean.[34] By comparison, the most desirable land in Sweden had been appropriated by the government for many centuries, so the land values there were high.[35]

Third, there was the impact of Gustaf Unonius, who immigrated in 1841 to Pine Lake, Wisconsin (today, near the town of Merton). He wrote letters to people in Sweden describing this voyage and the life in Pine Lake. He is often referred to as the first emigrant since there was almost no immigration to America prior to 1841.[36]

Finally, there was the pull of stories of earlier emigrants, beginning in the early 1840s, who had written letters back to their family and friends. Often their letters were published in one of the Swedish newspapers, such as the liberal *Aftonbladet*. These "American Letters" were a kind of subtle publicity, and as a result, a widespread chain reaction and contagion was set in motion. The number of emigrants exploded.[37]

During the 1850s, the number of Swedish immigrants to America averaged 1,690 per year. This increased to 12,245 per year by the 1870s. At that time, the Swedish crop failures and famine of 1867–1869 had an impact on many Swedes. In the 1880s, there were 57,000 per year—with a peak in 1888 of 45,000, the highest ever. Between 1891 and 1910, the number was 25,000 per year, and by the 1920s, it was 11,000 per year. One reason the Great Migration has been described as ending around 1940 was the fact that America put quotas in place for the number of immigrants that they would accept from specific countries, and their quota for Sweden gradually declined. In addition, there was the impact of the Great Depression.[38]

In Sweden, in 1870, some 72 percent of the population was engaged in agriculture or a related profession. By 1900, this figure had decreased to 52 percent. Sweden was slower to industrialize than many of the other European countries. As a result, wages in Sweden were comparatively low. Therefore, an overwhelming number of emigrants were people with farming background or at least a familiarity with rural life. For them, the desire for a better economic status was a huge factor in their decision to emigrate.[39] Sweden's population in 1800 was 2.4 million. The figure in the US in 1800 was 5.3 million.[40]

In the mid-1800s, the Swedish immigrants to America were mostly families with small children, but by the year 1900, some 75 percent of the immigrants were single people. The states in the US with the largest number of Swedish immigrants in 1880 were Illinois with forty-two thousand, Minnesota with thirty-nine thousand, and Iowa with eighteen thousand. In the early twentieth century, more Swedes lived in Chicago than in Gothenburg, Sweden's second largest city.[41]

Finally, for immigrants arriving in New York City, the opening of the Erie Canal in 1825 made it much easier for them to make the trip to the Midwest. The opening of Ellis Island to begin processing immigrants did not occur until

1892. Transatlantic travel by steamship began in about 1840 but wasn't popularized until about 1870.[42]

Illinois

When Erik and Charlotte left Sweden, they intended to land in Milwaukee and go 250 miles west to a place called Pine Lake, where some Swedes had settled (and about which Gustaf Unonius had written). Also, as mentioned earlier, as Erik, Charlotte, and Leonard traveled across the Great Lakes on the steamship *Klinton*, they were headed to the town of Southport, Illinois.

There was a town that was called Southport, but its name was changed in 1850 to Kenosha, Wisconsin—a town that is about sixty-five miles north of Chicago on Lake Michigan and also about seven miles north of the border between Illinois and Wisconsin.[43]

However, Erik explained the following:

> It was a seaman on the steamer who told us that we ought not to go to Milwaukee because there was no government land there to be gotten. He said he was well acquainted with all these regions. He said he could tell us where we could get land a few miles from the Lake near the southern boundary of Wisconsin, in northern Illinois. There was plenty of land there—and he told the truth. Consequently, we landed at Southport [now Kenosha, Wisconsin] and settled in northern Illinois, in Lake County.[44]

From Southport (now Kenosha), Erik and Charlotte went inland and eventually settled and bought land in a place that today is an unincorporated community called Rosecrans, Illinois—about thirteen miles southwest of Kenosha. We know this from the 1850 Census for Lake County, Illinois. It listed Erik as a forty-seven-year-old Swedish farmer, his wife, Charlotte, age forty-five, and their fifteen-year-old son, Leonard.[45]

We also now know the exact location of Erik and Charlotte's farm, thanks to a title search done by the Chicago Title Insurance Company in 1983. Their records show the two adjoining forty-acre lots that were purchased by Erik from the state of Illinois on September 17, 1843, and March 15, 1844, respectively.[46] Wisconsin had not yet been admitted as a state at that time, which explains why Erik had referred to the town of Southport, Illinois. The two lots today are wide-open, beautiful farmland.

Thomas Jefferson completed the Louisiana Purchase from France in 1803—effectively doubling the size of the United States. Two of the states that are featured in this book—Illinois and Wisconsin—were not part of the Louisiana Purchase. Illinois became a state in 1815, and Wisconsin became a state in 1848. The Lincoln-Douglas debates took place in 1858—one in each of the seven congressional districts in Illinois, except for Springfield and Chicago.[47] The election of Abe Lincoln of Illinois as president in 1860 and the Civil War from 1861 until 1865 were also significant events during this time.

Once Erik and Charlotte had arrived in the US and purchased their farm, Erik wrote a letter to his brother Pehr in Stockholm, describing his journey and how much it all cost and asking Pehr to please see that his letter was published in the *Aftonbladet* like the other America Letters that they had read before leaving Sweden.[48]

We also know from his letter that Erik had read about Gustaf Unonius and C. V. von Hauswolff, as he refers to them. Erik's letter was published on September 20, 1843. For many Swedish emigrants, the cost of the trip would not leave them with enough savings to purchase forty acres of land, so Erik and Charlotte were fortunate that they had a sufficient amount of savings.

Erik continued:

> Here we bought 40 acres of the best land for $1.50 per acre which was considered to be completely ample for my needs. I bought a pair of oxen for $30. I have already made several trips to the forest with them and brought home nine loads of hay.

> We built us a house and started farming with our steers. We got another cow and bought another 40 acres, cleared it, fenced it all and divided it into ten lots. It was hard work but I had a willing spirit and was gifted with energy so we worked through it and overcame many obstacles. By close calculation, we got mules and worked the land so that we obtained a season's premium for farming.

> My wife was very discontented during the first two years but she gradually became

as contented as anyone could be in our situation. I had to go out and work for others in order to help support us. I also had to split many rails. Afterwards, I bought ten acres of timber and paid 12 dollars an acre.[49]

Erik's wife, Charlotte, was "converted and united with the Baptist Church in Pleasant Prairie, Wisconsin [a town adjacent to Kenosha] in the year 1850"—seven years after they arrived there. Erik became a US citizen on March 11, 1852, in Lake County, Illinois.[50]

Erik wrote the following:

After we had labored in farming for 12 years, we rented out our farm for a year. I then worked for the Baptist Publication Society for one year—during 1855 and 1856. After that, we went to Chicago where we started with a little trade but it did not do very well so we quit after a year. Then, I served the First Baptist Church for part of that time as a Sexton. However, I quit when they sold their place of worship.

By 1864 [when Erik was age sixty-one], the United States Army had regained possession of most all of the rebel states. They found it necessary to establish societies to send out teachers to educate the African-American children. I made application to go somewhere, was commissioned and sent to

Vicksburg, Mississippi with two railroad
cars full of goods for the free men.[51]

Erik was probably working for the Freedmen's Bureau
that was established by President Lincoln as an important
agency in his reconstruction effort. This agency, which
reported to Union Army General Oliver Howard, was to
direct provisions, clothing, and fuel to those deemed to be
in need of immediate temporary shelter.

Erik continued:

> On April 2, 1864, I arrived there and
> delivered the goods. After this, I was sent to
> Louisiana—first to a plantation where they
> had a camp of about 800 African-American
> people. They had sent six teachers to this
> place—two men and four women. I became
> sick when I left Vicksburgh, Mississippi and
> arrived at Marshall's Plantation—or as it
> now was called, "Vanburens Hospital"—
> very exhausted and could not enter upon
> any duty for nearly two weeks.
>
> But after that time, I started my labors with
> energy and taught together with an old
> experienced schoolteacher—a Mrs. Polky
> from Chicago. The camp was broken up
> and we had to move to another camp on an
> island called "Paw Paw" in Louisiana. Here
> I began with a few Creole boys to teach
> the children. After a few days, I had 30
> students and was invited to join with Miss

Vitugusta [sic] Kimbal in a spacious room where we could teach together.

I learned a good many things from her. She was a devoted Christian but her health soon failed and I had to teach alone—somehow with 100 students. All the rest of the teachers left on account of ill health. I had the aching chills and fever. I prayed for strength to continue and finally overcame it all.

My wife arrived on November 8, 1864 [seven months after Erik had arrived there]. She took right hold with me in the school and we did get along well. At times, we had 130 students. More teachers came there from the Quakers. They were both willing and capable to take charge of the whole school so we handed it all over to them and left for Chicago on March 9, 1865—arriving on March 15th.

During my stay in the south [eleven months], I experienced many a blessing from the Lord especially in that I had the privilege to proclaim to them Christ and to instruct them more fully in the way of Godliness. Oh that the Lord will bless my soul and I believe that he will.

Buffalo, New York

Erik wrote the following:

> In the middle of May, we started for Buffalo,
> NY—where our son Leonard had been sent
> to open a branch of the coal business in
> 1864. I planned to join him as an Office
> Assistant.

> On September 13, 1866, my wife and I
> went from Buffalo to New York for a
> journey to Europe. We arrived at Hamburg
> on December 1st. [His passport application
> showed him as being 5' 8.5" and age sixty-
> three.][52] We travelled through Denmark
> and part of Sweden, arriving in Stockholm
> on December 10th where I met many of
> my old acquaintances and my sister, Anna
> Maglena.

> We stayed there for three months and
> had a very pleasant time. We then went
> to visit my brother Pehr's house on April
> 9, 1867 and found both him and my
> sister-in-law in good health. [His mother
> had apparently passed away by that time.]
> During my stay there, I had the privilege to
> testify of a survivor's love and by the means
> or instrument of winning some soles for
> Christ.[53]

After returning from Sweden, Erik and Charlotte lived in Buffalo. Charlotte died on December 19, 1877, at age seventy-one. Her obituary read, "At the time of her death, she was a member of the Prospect Avenue Baptist Church [in Buffalo] where she endeared herself to all. She had an utter simplicity of trust in Christ and a sense of absolute dependence upon God. The organization of women's mission circles in the Baptist churches of Buffalo was largely due to her agency. She was a faithful attendant upon all the services of the church."[54] Leonard's son, Arthur, said, "My grandmother I recall very slightly as a gentle, but very old lady with lace trimmings to her gown and a small piece of lace always on her hair."[55]

Meanwhile, Erik's son, Leonard, had set up his father in a small house close by, providing him with a housekeeper. Particulars are lacking, but the housekeeper was apparently married to Erik shortly thereafter.[56]

On August 23, 1890, Erik died at age eighty-seven. His grandson, Arthur Eric Hedstrom, said of his grandfather, "He was very aged, bent over somewhat and walked with a cane. When the Civil War broke out, he was appointed as Chaplain, in which capacity he served throughout the War. He and [his wife] were both extremely religious as were my parents [Leonard Hedstrom and his wife] and I recall family prayers held regularly each day immediately after breakfast."[57]

Looking Back

Erik first started to write his diary in Chicago in 1860. He began by saying, "58 years of my life have passed and nothing yet written down concerning my life. However unimportant it may appear to some (I never expect that it will come to any publicity), it has been of importance to me and I will leave it [the diary] as a memory to my son."[58]

Erik lived until the age of eighty-seven, a long life span in the nineteenth century, and had been married to his wife for forty-three years. Their marriage was apparently a successful one. Erik and Charlotte lived long enough to see their only child, Leonard, grow up, attend college, marry, and live very much the American dream of rags to riches. In fact, his son, Leonard, attended the University of Rochester in Rochester, New York—a campus that Erik and Charlotte would have seen when they traveled across the Eric Canal in 1843.

Both Erik and Charlotte had many friends in Stockholm whom they were able to go back and see again many years after they left Sweden for America. Erik also managed to visit his mother nine years after leaving during his trip to Stockholm. By that time, he had established himself as a shoemaker.

Erik's wife, Charlotte, must have found the first few years in America to be very difficult—not knowing the English language, starting on a farm out in the middle of the US, and with her husband working hard every day to try to make ends meet. She found the Baptist Church to be a source of great comfort and spiritual inspiration for the rest of her life. She must have been very proud of her son, Leonard, and all that he accomplished. She also must have enjoyed seeing many of her old friends when she and Erik visited Sweden toward the end of her life.

When the *Swedish Pioneer Historical Quarterly* published Erik's letter to his brother Pehr in 1981, the editor of that periodical referred to Erik's letter as being "one of the very earliest preserved Swedish 'America Letters' from the 19th century, having been written a couple of years before the great emigration from Sweden got properly underway … it reveals a remarkably well-informed, widely travelled, and independent-minded man …"[59]

Erik worked very hard at manual labor—both as a shoemaker and as a farmer. He and his wife were deeply religious people. Erik lost his father just after his sixth birthday, and as a young boy, he had witnessed war, famine, poverty, and much hardship in the north of Sweden. By the end of his life, he must have been quite proud of all he had accomplished.

Photographs for Chapter One

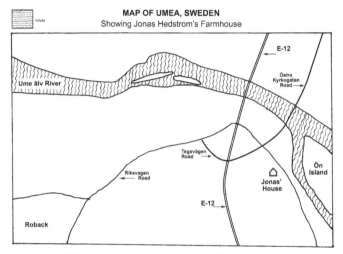

Map of Umea showing the location of Jonas Hedstrom's farmhouse. The twelve parcels of land he owned were all located within a few hundred yards of the farmhouse, although they were not all contiguous. See acknowledgments.

Photo is believed to be of Erik Hedstrom—
taken while he was traveling in Germany.

Photo of Erik Hedstrom's farm in northern
Illinois, taken by the author in about 1985.

Erik Hedstrom Farm in Northern Illinois

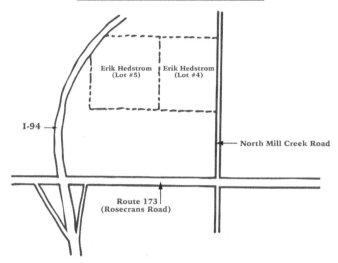

Map showing directions to Erik Hedstrom's farm in Illinois. Coming from Chicago (fifty miles) north on I-94, take exit #2 for Rt. 173/ Rosecrans Road. Turn right at end of exit ramp onto Rt. 173 and go about half a mile. Then turn left on North Mill Creek Road and watch on your left after about a quarter mile. Lot 5 purchased in September 1843, and Lot 4 purchased in March 1844.

Christina Charlotta (Fritz) Hedstrom
(1806–1877)

Chapter Two

ERIC L. HEDSTROM
(1835–1894)

> The farther back you can look, the farther
> forward you are likely to see.

SIR WINSTON CHURCHILL (1874–1965)

Eric Leonard Hedstrom
("Leonard")

In June 1885, Leonard Hedstrom was on one of his many trips to Chicago to see what was going on with his business interests there.[1] Several years earlier, he had become a partner of a coal and iron merchant based in Chicago, called A. B. Meeker, and had opened up their office in Buffalo, New York. By now, Leonard had established his own company—called the E. L. Hedstrom Company. It was in the business of distributing anthracite coal, a tremendous business. His company was selling coal all over western New York, on west to Chicago, and way out in the Dakotas, Wisconsin, Iowa, and Nebraska. Leonard had become the largest shipper of coal on the Great Lakes. In addition to coal distribution, the company was now mixed up with coal mining and with the making of pig iron.

When he arrived in Chicago on this particular trip, Leonard discovered, much to his horror, that his business partner had made off with a very large amount of funds. Steps were taken at once to track down the misappropriated funds that had almost all been invested in Chicago waterfront real estate. The deeds were located, and the parcels of land were transferred to E. L. Hedstrom & Co. As a result of all of this, the business partnership was dissolved. The E. L. Hedstrom Company was subsequently divided into two parts; one was called E. L. Hedstrom—Chicago, and the other was called E. L. Hedstrom—Buffalo. The business of these companies continued to grow until they reached their peak of moneymaking and then declined with the changing times.[2]

Sweden and Illinois

Leonard Hedstrom had been born at Baggensgatan 21 in the block Perseus in Old Stockholm, Sweden, on August 21, 1835. He was the only child of shoemaker Erik Hedstrom and his wife, Charlotte.[3] As we know from the prior chapter, Erik, Charlotte, and Leonard sailed on the *Hindoo* from Stockholm to New York City in 1843 when Leonard was seven years old. They settled on their own farm in northern Illinois. The 1850 US Census referred to Leonard as then being a fifteen-year old who was at school in Newport township in Lake County, Illinois. This county now covers an area of about 444 square miles. It includes several towns and cities and also the property where Erik and Charlotte had their eighty-acre farm.

Leonard's father, Erik, had written this in his diary:

> Our son, who was eight years old when
> we arrived, has grown up but did not feel

inclined to be a farmer. He first decided to learn the blacksmith trade. He started with this and kept at it for about a year in the city of Waukegan, Illinois [about twelve miles southeast of where Erik had his farm]. During that time, he changed his mind and decided to give up his trade and begin a course of study.

After two years, he went to the University of Rochester in Rochester, NY for his studies. [The University's campus is near the Erie Canal]. But then Leonard's health failed him and he came home. After he had gotten better, he graduated at a commercial college in Chicago.[4]

In 1856 Leonard, who was then about age twenty-one, found a position with A. B. Meeker, a Chicago-based independent coal operator and large pig iron merchant. He initially worked there as a bookkeeper.[5] After a few years, he was made a partner. Although Abe Lincoln was becoming a well-known political figure in Illinois during the 1850s, particularly with the Lincoln-Douglas debates that took place in different locations throughout the state of Illinois, Erik did not make any reference to President Lincoln in his diary.

Buffalo, New York

In 1864, Leonard was sent by the firm to Buffalo, New York, to open an office there. While in Buffalo, he attended the Cedar Street Baptist Church, where he met a young woman named Anna Matilda Clampffer. The chemistry between these two must have been quite strong, as we have two letters that Leonard wrote to Anna, dated December 12, 1864, and April 25, 1865. In the second letter, he proposes that they get married—which they eventually did in Buffalo at the home of W. H. Case, Esq., on July 6, 1865. Then they got married again in Chicago in Cook County on July 11, 1865—probably where some of Leonard's friends could attend.[6] He was then age twenty-nine, and Anna was twenty-eight. One thing they had in common was that they were both only children.

Anna Clampffer had been born in Reading, Pennsylvania, on June 29, 1837. Her parents were William W. and Ann Elizabeth Clampffer. We believe that her ancestors were originally from Holland. Her father passed away when Anna was only about three years old. Her mother had moved several times, but she and Anna ended up in Buffalo in 1855. Anna had been a coeditor of her school newspaper. She joined the Cedar Street Baptist Church in 1862.[7]

After Leonard and Anna were married, they moved into a house on Michigan Street between Seneca and Swan. Their daughter, Alice, was born there on April 14, 1866 [nine months and eight days after their Buffalo marriage]. Their next house was on North Division Street, where their son, Arthur Eric, was born on August 6, 1869. Later that year, they moved into 84 Seventh Street.[8]

Leonard's grandson, Eric Douglas, wrote this:

> Several things of interest happened while at Seventh Street: Erik and Charlotte had gone abroad and returned; Erik has become an "office assistant" to his son in his growing coal business in Buffalo; and Leonard's mother Charlotte died in Buffalo in December 1877.

> The [coal] business was growing all this time—the Chicago fire took away a large part of the city in 1871 but nothing was recorded as to damage to Meeker's property. Leonard was becoming more a man of importance, his interests other than business centering on the church, the Y.M.C.A. and other civic endeavors.

> In 1882, [Leonard] built the house at 717 Delaware Avenue, between North and Summer Streets. [After he died, his wife, Anna, continued to] live there until the mid-1920s.

> Leonard must have been very strict. The new house was quite large and contained on the third floor, one huge room with an adjoining kitchen. Up here, large church functions took place and it seems that although Leonard and Anna were

teetotalers, crème de menthe was usually served after supper.

Alcohol was a horror, so much so that Leonard would not permit coal orders to be filled with the local breweries. Mr. Eugene Roberts, then a young salesman, specialized in this type of trade and was threatened with dismissal if he continued to solicit these accounts. Mr. Roberts told me that a special sheet was kept in the monthly sales report showing no breweries but very handsome purchases under a fake name that were not questioned. Business grew and grew. Mr. Roberts said these brewery orders were the biggest accounts on the books and without them he would have starved to death.[9]

Meanwhile, shortly after setting up the office of A. B. Meeker in Buffalo, Leonard set up his own company at the foot of Erie Street. Leonard began receiving coal from New York by canal and transferring it to sailing vessels at Peck Slip. In 1866, he moved to what later became known as the Salt Dock on the Blackwell Canal, and he also handled smaller quantities at a small dock in the Erie Basin.

The shipping of anthracite coal on the lakes began when lake vessels were loaded with coal brought in by canal, the boats coming not only from Seneca and Cayuga Lakes in the middle of New York state but also from the Hudson River district that had canal connection with the anthracite mines. Some coal came from the Jersey waterfront at Perth Amboy.

The anthracite interests had now developed a business in Buffalo that required much improvement and enlargement of facilities for the handling of coal. Leonard was one of the most active in initiating and instituting improvements in shipping conditions.

A review of the earliest conditions of lake shipment of coal shows that the methods were primitive. "Coal was for a number of years transferred to lake boats by wheelbarrows or buckets; in fact this method was used until the large coal shipping trestles were erected."

Leonard took the initiative in about 1870 by building the Buffalo Creek railway. He was president of that enterprise until it was taken over by the Lehigh Valley and Erie Companies in about 1876. For five years or more after coming to Buffalo, Leonard was the representative of the Lehigh Valley Company for coal sales. Jointly with the Lehigh Valley Railway Company, Leonard erected in 1871 the first coal trestle in Buffalo at the Lehigh Docks, on Buffalo Creek, for the transfer of anthracite coal from cars to vessels. It was used until about 1883, when a new trestle, built opposite the Blackwell Canal, was completed. Other shippers then started trestle building. Leonard was appointed general western sales agent for the handling and sales of Scranton coal for the Lehigh Valley Company in 1870.

Leonard severed his relationship with Lehigh in 1876, and after about two years spent in managing the coal-shipping interests of the Erie Company at Buffalo, he formed an alliance with the Delaware, Lackawanna, and Western

(DL&W) to handle their coal distribution almost exclusively. The firm of E. L. Hedstrom was then the only individual shipper of anthracite coal from Buffalo by lake to the upper lake ports. Also, the extensive docks of the Hedstrom firm in South Chicago and other points in the market indicate a large level of activity in the western anthracite trade. This relationship with the DL&W remained intact for the rest of Leonard's life and was continued thereafter by the firm he had founded. Leonard's Buffalo office was then located at 304–312 Ellicott Square. In 1879, Leonard sold his interest in the Buffalo Creek Railway to the Erie Railroad.

In 1880, Leonard also began handling and distributing various grades of bituminous (or soft) coal the first Pittsburgh coal in the Buffalo market. At that time, Leonard built and operated the first steam coal fueling lighter used in the Buffalo Harbor. Other fueling companies soon adopted the same device that they found to be very convenient for fueling steamers when loading and unloading cargoes.

By the mid-1880s, the Chicago office was called Meeker, Hedstrom & Co, with offices at 95 Dearborn Street. Then, by 1888, the Chicago office was called E. L. Hedstrom & Co, and there were three partners: E.L. Hedstrom, G. W. Meeker, and J. H. Brown. At that time, the firm had three offices—in Chicago, Buffalo, and Racine, Wisconsin. In Chicago, their office was at 115 Dearborn Street. In addition to being a wholesale dealer in coal, the firm was also distributing coke and iron.[10]

Business, Civic, and Religious Organizations

Leonard was also quite involved in various business, civic, religious, and charitable organizations. In terms of business organizations, he was an active member of the Buffalo Board of Trade and served as the president of the Buffalo Merchant's Exchange in 1884 and 1885.[11] He was also a director of the Buffalo Bank of Commerce.

Leonard's involvement in religious organizations included his serving as president of the Buffalo Baptist Union for many years. Two Baptist churches in Buffalo benefitted from Leonard's generosity. First, the Delaware Avenue Baptist Church was opened for services at 965 Delaware Avenue in January 1895, the year after Leonard passed away. This church was only a block or two from Leonard's house on Delaware Avenue. Before he died, he made significant donations to that church. As a result, this church records state that "the pipe organ, pulpit platform and baptistery are a memorial to Eric Leonard Hedstrom."[12] Second, the Hedstrom Memorial Baptist Church was founded in 1895, also the year after Leonard passed away. This church was originally located at 165 Doat Street and then moved to 1720 Wehrle Drive in Amherst, New York. Leonard also involved with the Rochester Theological Seminary.

Leonard served as president of the YMCA from 1871 until 1876, as a director of the Buffalo Homeopathic Hospital and of the Homestead Lodging House (part of the Christian Homestead Association) that was located at 84 Lloyd Street. His wife, Anna, was very involved with a nursing home then called the Home for the Friendless, located at 1500 Main Street in Buffalo. The name of this home was later changed to the Bristol Home.[13]

Leonard's son, Arthur, said, "My father's only interest outside of business and philanthropy was his fondness for horses"[14] (probably from growing up on the family farm in Illinois before the invention of automobiles).

Trip to Sweden

In 1894, Leonard and Anna left for Sweden, although Leonard had not been well physically for the prior two years. His passport application, dated 1893, indicated that at that time, Leonard was 5'10". On this trip, they were accompanied by two maids.[15]

On August 6, they visited Drottningholm Palace—about four miles west of Stockholm—where they met the king of Sweden.[16]

Eric Douglas (Leonard's grandson) wrote this:

> While in Sweden, they purchased two grandfather clocks and a wonderful single horse, two-passenger sleigh with a driver's seat high above and back of the main seat. On the return from abroad aboard the *Teutonic*, an illness overcame Leonard. He was not very old [fifty-nine years] but the disease baffled the best of doctors. He was taken from the ship, rushed to a special train and hurried to Buffalo where he died not long after in his home [on October 13, 1894].[17]

Leonard's son, Arthur, said of his father, "He had devoted the greater part of his life to the service of others and had absolutely worn himself out."[18] On Leonard's grave marker in Buffalo, it quotes the Bible, Revelation 14:13: "They may rest from their labors, and their works follow them."

Leonard's wife, Anna, lived another thirty-four years until the age of ninety-one, most of that time in the family's house at 717 Delaware Avenue, along with "two domestics" according to the 1920 census. Mary Warren, who married Leonard and Anna's grandson, said that she had been in the house at 717 Delaware Avenue once. She described it as being dark and not cheerful. Anna Hedstrom died on May 2, 1929, apparently while asleep. At that time, she was living in an apartment at Park Lane in Buffalo. A brief funeral service was conducted for her in the chapel at the Forest Lawn Cemetery in Buffalo by her pastor at the Delaware Avenue Baptist Church.[19]

Looking Back

It is interesting how the original voyage by seven-year-old Leonard across the Erie Canal and then across the Great Lakes to the Chicago area influenced his decision of where to attend college and also the business of shipping coal on the Great Lakes between Buffalo and Chicago—coal that in some cases was shipped to Buffalo via the Eric Canal.

Although he only lived to be fifty-nine years old, he lived a full life. His marriage to Anna lasted twenty-nine years. Together they had two children. Alice eventually attended a finishing school in Philadelphia and was married to William

Douglas. He had attended law school at Columbia University and was working as a law clerk in the office of Grover Cleveland (later President Cleveland) in Buffalo. The second child was Arthur, who attended a private school in Buffalo and then graduated from the University of Rochester, where Leonard had also studied. Arthur would eventually take over his father's various business interests. Leonard had lived to see his daughter, Alice, married and to see her daughter, Anne, born—his granddaughter. However, he did not live to see Alice's second child born or to see his son, Arthur, get married.

Leonard achieved a considerable amount of success as a businessman. He contributed significantly to his community in the Buffalo area—both to the Baptist Church and to various civic organizations such as the YMCA. At the time of his death, he left everything he owned to his wife outright. Many years later, she then left everything she owned to her two children outright, equally. Alice and Arthur both went on to marry and have children and grandchildren.

Photographs for Chapter Two

Leonard Hedstrom as a young man.

Leonard Hedstrom as a young man.

Anna Matilda Clampffer
(1837–1929)

House of Leonard and Anna Hedstrom at 717
Delaware Avenue in Buffalo, New York.

Chapter Three

ARTHUR E. HEDSTROM
(1869–1946)

Ancestor worship in ancient China dates back to the Neolithic period [6000 to 1000 BC] and it would prove to be the most popular and enduring Chinese religious practice, lasting well into modern times. The family was always an important concept in Chinese society and government, and it was maintained by the twin pillars of filial piety and respect for one's dead ancestors.

ANCIENT HISTORY ENCYCLOPEDIA (2017)

Arthur Eric Hedstrom
("Arthur")

On the second day after Arthur and Katherine arrived in Cannes, France, in 1901, they stopped by the Golf Club and, by chance, met Grand Duke Michael (Mikhailovich) and his wife, Countess de Torby. Grand Duke Michael was a grandson of Tsar Nicholas I of Russia. The four of them ended up playing golf together, and as Arthur later said, "This accidental meeting led to an intimate and lasting friendship and opened every social avenue to us" in Cannes.[1]

Arthur and Katherine rented an apartment in the Californie residential neighborhood for three consecutive winter seasons, beginning in 1901.[2] This neighborhood sits about one and a half miles from the center of Cannes, up on a hillside with spectacular views of the city and the bay below.

Arthur was originally drawn to Cannes because it had one of the few golf courses in that part of Europe. This course, now known as the Cannes-Mandelieu Old Race Golf Course, is the oldest golf course on the French Riviera. It was built in 1891 by Grand Duke Michael of Russia. Arthur said that the social life in Cannes "was distinctively among the villas and the two very exclusive clubs—le Circle Nautique and le Circle d'Union."[3]

The various experiences that Arthur and Katherine had during those three winters led Arthur to write a novel about it called *Call Me Sonja*, which was published many years later.[4]

Arthur's Early Years

Arthur Hedstrom was born in Buffalo, New York, on August 8, 1869, the second of two children of Leonard and Anna Hedstrom. At the time he was born, his parents were living on Michigan Street near Swan Street.[5]

In 1882, when Arthur was thirteen, his parents moved into their new house at 717 Delaware Avenue. Arthur attended the Heathcote School for Boys in Buffalo, a small private school on 310 Pearl Street that was "under the protection of the Episcopal Church." He then attended the Briggs School in Buffalo before attending the University of Rochester, where he graduated from in 1892. Arthur later referred to his performance at school as being "perfunctory."[6]

After his freshman year in college, he said, "My scholastic standing was somewhat questioned especially in languages, so my father thought it might be good for me to go to Heidelberg for the summer to study German. My sister and I went abroad and settled in Heidelberg for the greater part of our stay. We lived with a German family, but I am afraid I spent most of my time with the University students who spoke English."[7]

While he was away at college, Arthur's grandfather Erik passed away. Then, after Arthur graduated from college, his father, Leonard, passed away in 1894 when Arthur was twenty-five. Eric Douglas, Arthur's nephew, said that "after his father's death, [Arthur] stepped into the business."[8] The business interests of his father, at the time of his death, consisted of being the acting partner of the firm E. L. Hedstrom & Company in Buffalo and Chicago and also president of the Franklin Iron Manufacturing Company.

It would be a few years before he would be married, and during that time, he must have been quite a figure in Buffalo. It is said that he had a very fine high wheel cart for two—very smart—which he drove tandem (two horses, one in front of the other). His sister said, "As a young man, he wore the highest collars, the gayest of ties and the very longest of overcoats—always the latest cloth and style."[9]

During the years after Arthur graduated from university (1892) until he was married (1898), he took several trips. On one, he and a friend traveled from New York to San Francisco by water—before the Panama Canal was built. They stopped in Panama and Costa Rica. On another, in 1895, he and another friend went to the Mediterranean, visiting Genoa, Italy, and Monte Carlo.[10]

Arthur was an unusually gifted athlete. Although he had played first base on the University of Rochester baseball team, his two big sports were golf and tennis. In his autobiography, Arthur listed ninety-five golf courses in the US and fifty-three courses in nine other countries on which he had played. He was, at one time, responsible for the golf activities at the Buffalo Country Club and also managed to become the Buffalo City champion in golf. Within the family, it was known that he was an unusually good golfer. For example, he won the Buffalo Country Club Championship in November 1896.[11]

In tennis, Arthur managed to play in the finals in the Buffalo City Championship in singles for three different years. In tennis doubles, he and his partner, Harold Meadows, were Western New York champions. He also played polo for two years at the Buffalo Country Club but said he played that sport rather indifferently.

There were two games that Arthur enjoyed playing—bridge and billiards. In bridge, he and Frank Alderman won the Buffalo City Auction Bridge Tournament in 1924. In billiards, he played on teams at both the Saturn and the Buffalo Clubs.

Arthur and Katherine

Arthur wrote in his autobiography, "The outstanding event in my life and one that has brought undreamed of happiness was the meeting of a young girl named Katherine Meigs Wilcox."[12] She was born on August 13, 1875, in New Haven, Connecticut, the youngest of ten children of Daniel Hand Wilcox Sr. and Francis Louisa Ansley. At the time they met, Katherine was teaching "physical training" at the Buffalo Seminary School in Buffalo. She was apparently a good athlete and was quite good at both golf and tennis.

Katherine's family lived in New Haven until 1896, when they moved to Buffalo. Daniel Wilcox was from an old New England family, while his wife, Francis, was originally from Augusta, Georgia. As a young girl, Katherine attended Rosemary Hall, a boarding school that was then in Greenwich, Connecticut. She was also a Girl Scout.[13]

Arthur and Katherine were married on June 14, 1898, at the home of Katherine's brother, Ansley Wilcox, a prominent attorney in Buffalo. Their marriage took place in the same room that Theodore Roosevelt was sworn in as president about two years later. Arthur was then age twenty-eight, and Katherine was twenty-two. They spent their honeymoon "in England driving with a coach and four from one golf course to another."

The young married couple rented an apartment at 27 Oakland Place, perhaps one of the nicest streets in the main residential area of Buffalo. While they were living there, their first of three children, a son named Eric Leonard, was born on March 12, 1899. Then they moved to a house at 498 Delaware Avenue, where their daughter, Brenda, was born on September 20, 1902. Meanwhile, they spent summers on Grand Island in a house that was adjoining the Falconwood Club. This club was a resort for several of the wealthy families of Buffalo. Arthur served as president of the club for several years.

Arthur and Alice were very active on the social circuit in Buffalo. They were members of many of Buffalo's nicest clubs, including the Buffalo Club, the Saturn Club, the Buffalo Athletic Club, the Buffalo Country Club, and the Buffalo Tennis and Squash Club.

At this time, when they had young children, they decided

to take several trips abroad. The first was a trip in 1900 to the Grand Canyon and Mexico in a private railroad car that a friend had loaned to Arthur. (This adventure featured in his novel, *Call Me Sonja*.) Five others joined them on this trip.[14] When they got to Mexico, Katherine and three others climbed the volcanic mountain called Popocatepetl, which is about forty-three miles southwest of Mexico City, to the top so that they could look down into the crater. At 17,802 feet, it is the second highest mountain in Mexico and is very much an active volcano.[15] Then Arthur and Katherine spent three consecutive winters in Cannes, France, from 1901 to 1903 (Arthur was thirty-two, and Katherine was twenty-six.)

Four Winds Farm

In 1904, they purchased ninety-seven acres of land located at what was then 4200 Main Street in Eggartsville, New York (now 4196 Main Street in Amherst, New York, between Four Winds Way and Getzville Road), where they built a home in 1906. This was about eight miles from downtown Buffalo. They purchased an additional ten acres for that property in 1922, built the gatehouses in 1907, a tennis court in 1915, a swimming pool, and bathhouses in 1921.[16]

Their son Lars was born on August 21, 1909. Meanwhile, these years were spent developing their property into a beautiful country estate with a tennis court, a swimming pool, bathhouses, a barn, formal gardens, and a pond. Initially, they had thoughts of making this a working farm with four milk cows and two heavy workhorses to plow the fields. For about ten years, they employed a farmer named

Mr. Ball to help with the work, which Katherine apparently supervised, before they gave up on the idea of running a real farm. In the gatehouse at the entrance of the property were two apartments. The one on the left as one entered was used for Mr. Ball and then later for Aunt Mable, Katherine's older sister. Years later, this apartment was used by Arthur's son, Eric Sr., and his wife, Mary. The other gatehouse apartment was used for Charles Tong, the chauffer. Aunt Mable apparently had a broken love affair and never married. She read a lot, according to one family member. Her politics were Democratic, as opposed to Arthur and Katherine, who were Republicans. Arthur and Katherine's daughter, Brenda, also settled on the Four Winds Farm property, building a house with her husband, William Boocock. This made the farm into sort of a family compound.

Arthur and Katherine didn't get into Buffalo for social occasions as much when they were living at the Four Winds Farm, although they did attend church on Sundays at the Delaware Avenue Baptist Church. After church, they would usually have lunch with Arthur's mother, Anna, who the family referred to as "little granny." They also entertained quite often at Four Winds Farm, although Katherine missed being closer to the social life in Buffalo.[17]

At the outbreak of WWI in 1914, Arthur said that he went to the Mexican border with Troop One.[18] Meanwhile, Katherine became increasingly involved in Republican politics. During the period from 1920 until 1933, there was a constitutional ban on the production, import, transportation, and sale of alcoholic beverages in the US. However, many people continued to drink in spite of the ban—so much so that anyone who was a Prohibitionist was often put in an awkward and unpopular position. Leonard and Anna had been Prohibitionists, as were Arthur and Katherine.[19]

Children

Eric, Brenda, and Lars all grew up spending most of their childhood years on the Four Winds Farm property. Eric had attended the Franklin School and the Nichols School, both private schools in Buffalo, before going away to the Hill School, a boarding school in Pottstown, Pennsylvania. Then he attended Yale University.[20]

Brenda attended the Franklin School, the Park School, and the Buffalo Seminary, all private schools in Buffalo, before going away to the Westover boarding school in Middlebury, Connecticut. She had her coming-out party at the Buffalo Country Club. Lars attended the Franklin School and the Nichols School in Buffalo before going away to Hotchkiss, a boarding school in Lakeville, Connecticut. Then he attended Princeton University.

In the early days, Arthur would ride tandem in a horse-drawn cart down Delaware Avenue, which was then a smooth dirt street. However, when automobiles became popular, Arthur would have his chauffer, Charles Tong, take him to work in Buffalo in his maroon Pierce-Arrow limousine. During the day, he would often go to the Buffalo Club for lunch and occasionally a game of bridge. Katherine and each of the children were given cars. For example, Brenda got a Cadillac for her eighteenth birthday.[21]

Arthur's Business Career

Having stepped into his father's business interests when Arthur was twenty-five, he managed to continue to grow the coal distribution business for many years. The E. L. Hedstrom business eventually had coal trestles in five locations in Buffalo: at the foot of Erie Street; at Chicago and Miami Streets; at North Main Street and the DL & W railroad; at Walden Avenue and the DL & W railroad; and in the Blackrock area at East and Parish Streets. The company also maintained coal yards: at Delaware Avenue and the DL & W railroad; at Erie Street; at Walden Avenue; at Chicago Street and in the Blackrock area. There was also a soft coal yard at Roseville and Van Rensselaer Streets. The company was mining and shipping bituminous coal and coke, "smokeless coal," "Smithing Coal," "Gas and Steam Coal," and the DL & W's Scranton Coal.[22]

In 1927 (when Arthur was about fifty-eight years old), the E. L. Hedstrom Co in Buffalo merged with Spaulding & Spaulding, another Buffalo coal company owned by two brothers—Stephen Van Rensselaer Spaulding and Elbridge Spaulding. The resulting company was known as the Hedstrom-Spaulding Coal Company. It was to continue for another twenty-eight years until it was merged with Henry Yates's coal company in Buffalo in 1955—with the successor company being called Spaulding-Yates.[23]

Later, Arthur became president of the Fairmont Coal Company, the Duth Hill Mining Company, the Snyder Gas Company, Cooper Paper Box Company, the Oak Ridge & Bostonia Railroad, the Hedstrom Holding Company, and Hedstrom-Spaulding, Inc. as well as a director of other companies.[24] Arthur purchased the Cooper Paper Box Company as a means of diversifying out of the coal business because he thought the coal distribution business was beginning to go into a long-term decline. Arthur's oldest son, Eric Sr., eventually became president of the Cooper Paper Box Company.[25]

Arthur's Religious and Civic Involvement

In 1913, when Arthur was about forty-four, he helped organize the Buffalo Federation of Churches, a group of representatives of forty-eight churches and eleven denominations. He was elected the first president of this organization.[26] Arthur was for many years a member of the Delaware Avenue Baptist Church. He and his wife also helped organize the Amherst Community Church.

Arthur was a director of the YMCA in Buffalo from 1900 until 1926 and on its board of trustees from 1920 until 1932. He was a life member of the Albright Art Gallery and the Buffalo Public Library in Buffalo. In 1910, Arthur worked with a friend to organize and build "The Men's Hotel," an inexpensive but good lodging house for men and boys. He then organized a campaign for the building of "The Girls' Home." Arthur served as the treasurer for the Rent Fund of the Salvation Army. He also rented a building and equipped it as a Social Center for African Americans. Then, in 1928, he and a friend built a model apartment house for African Americans who had large families. For this apartment building, they charged a "moderate rental."[27]

Buffalo's mayor appointed Arthur to the school board in about 1900. Arthur also served as sole trustee of the school in Snyder, New York, for about seven years. In politics, Arthur served as a member of the electoral college for Teddy Roosevelt's Progressive Party.

Katherine's Activities

Katherine had been active in civic and women's affairs for many years. She was an organizer of the Girl Scouts in Buffalo during WWI. Katherine taught Sunday school at the Delaware Baptist Church. She was connected with the women's suffrage movement and the Joint Charities. For seventeen years, she served on the board of directors of the YWCA.

A prominent prohibitionist, Katherine at one time wrote a column on the editorial page of the *Buffalo Times*. In another article in a local magazine, *Leader Militant*, in July 1931, Katherine is referred to as having the reputation of being "the only prohibitionist 'hereabouts,'" perhaps because she was the publicity director of the Citizens Committee for Law Enforcement, a Prohibitionist group.[28] In June 1951, Katherine sent letters to President Truman, Secretary of State Dean Acheson, and General Eisenhower suggesting a plan to end the Korean War. A member of General Eisenhower's staff sent a nice note acknowledging her letter.

Arthur's Inheritance

When his mother passed away in May 1929, Arthur (then about age sixty) inherited his one half share of her estate.[29] He and Katherine went back to Cannes, France—then about twenty-five years from when they had spent three winters there. Grand Duke Mikael and his wife had died, and the nameplates on many of the well-known villas had new names they didn't recognize. In the place where the Circle d' Union once stood, there was nothing there but old memories.

However, when Arthur went over to the golf course and walked up to the front door, he was called by name. He looked up and recognized the golf professional—"the only one in Cannes who remembers me," he said.[30]

Travel for Winters

Arthur and Katherine loved to travel. They took their winter holidays almost every year in various different places to escape the harsh Buffalo winters. The places they visited included "Laurel in the Pines," a horsey resort in Lakewood, New Jersey; Palm Beach, Florida; Pinehurst, North Carolina; Augusta, Georgia; and many other resorts. In 1935, they rented a house in Bermuda for the winter, where they entertained family members and friends. Toward the end of Arthur's life, they were spending their winters at the Riomar Country Club in Vero Beach, Florida.[31]

Arthur and Katherine got a bit of the flying bug when it became possible to travel by airplane. They flew from Hawaii to San Francisco and from Bermuda to the New

York City area. They apparently had tickets for the first transatlantic commercial flight that was to leave in 1937.[32]

Arthur and Katherine Pass Away

Arthur died in Vero Beach, Florida, on February 24, 1946, at the age of seventy-six. Two years later, the family sold the E. L. Hedstrom—Chicago company. Fortunately, the family had held on to the waterfront real estate for years, so it was eventually sold for "tremendous prices," according to Eric Douglas, one of his grandsons.[33]

Katherine died in Buffalo on June 26, 1952, at the age of seventy-six. By coincidence, she died while her grandson Eric Hedstrom Jr. was visiting her for lunch in her apartment at 900 Delaware Avenue. The Four Winds Farm had been sold some years earlier. During the year after she died, the family sold their interest in the E. L. Hedstrom—Buffalo company.[34]

Looking Back

Arthur and Katherine led a very glamorous life with many of the nicest trappings of wealth. They were married for forty-seven years and got to know each of their six grandchildren—three boys and three girls. Arthur had achieved business, social, and community prominence. Arthur was fortunate to inherit the job of managing a significant business from his father and, at the age of sixty, a large inheritance from his mother. Nevertheless, he managed to grow the nest egg that he inherited significantly by the time he passed away at the age of seventy-six.[35] He was deeply involved in many civic and religious activities and organizations. He was an unusually good-looking man and a truly gifted athlete—someone who certainly had an awful lot going for him.

Arthur's wife, Katherine, was a woman with her own independent thoughts—in politics and in her efforts to give back to the community. Her daughter, Brenda, described her mother by saying, "She loved music and the theater; she was basically a culturally minded person who enjoyed all the arts; [she] painted and played the piano; [she had] a buoyant and happy nature."[36]

Brenda described her father, Arthur, by saying, "He was a far more serious nature but he had a twinkle in his blue eyes and a most gracious and gallant manner—which endeared him to all women—sometimes to mother's annoyance; He was a most fastidious man in his personal appearance and in his choice of what he wore; He had all his suits custom-made; He dressed for dinner every night [when Arthur and Katherine] slowly sipped their one small glass of sherry sitting before the huge fireplace; He was a perfect and true gentleman."[37]

Arthur decided to write and privately publish his autobiography in 1937 (when he was sixty-nine). A significant portion of this small thirty-two-page book was devoted to listing all the golf courses on which he had played and to describing the social life during his winters in Cannes. However, as anyone who has played quite a bit of golf knows, to achieve the level of play that Arthur achieved requires an enormous level of mental discipline.

Photographs for Chapter Three

Arthur Hedstrom as a young man.

Katherine Meigs (Wilcox) Hedstrom
(1875–1952)

Alice Charlotte Hedstrom
(She married William A. Douglas)

Four Winds Farm, Buffalo, New York
(View of main house from gardens behind house.)

The gatehouse at entrance of Four Winds Farm.

Arthur Hedstrom often rode tandem down
Delaware Avenue in Buffalo, New York.

Chapter Four

ERIC L. HEDSTROM SR.
PHOTO OF HIM STANDING IN FRONT OF
THE HOUSE WHERE HE AND HIS WIFE,
ETHEL, LIVED IN DARIEN, CONNECTICUT
(1899–1961).

Gentility is what is left over from rich
ancestors after the money is gone.

JOHN CIARDI (1916–1986)

Eric Leonard Hedstrom
("Eric Sr.")

It was a warm afternoon on June 8, 1921. The wedding
of Eric Sr. and Mary Warren at the Crescent Avenue
Presbyterian Church in Plainfield, New Jersey, was
presided over by two ministers—the former pastor and
the current pastor. The organ music was "an attractive
program of classical selections followed by Mendelssohn's
Wedding March as the bridal party entered the church. The
decorations were most attractive, comprised of pink rambler
roses, delphinium and white stock, all arranged in a pleasing
manner. The bride was gowned in cream white satin with a
train of old family lace and she carried a shower bouquet of
lilies of the valley," according to the local newspaper.[1] The
reception was held at the house of Mary's family at 966
Hillside Avenue in Plainfield.

The couple had gotten engaged about four months
earlier. While at Yale, Eric Sr. had become friends with
Robert Stevens, who brought him back to visit his family

in Plainfield. During that time, he introduced Eric to a family friend, Mary Warren. Mary's notes describe her initial impression on meeting Eric Sr. as "very entrancing."[2]

Mary Warren

Mary Warren attended the Hartridge School in Plainfield until 1916. She had learned how to play the piano, and she taught two Sunday school classes, one that was "at a poor mission." Her coming-out party was at the Plainfield Country Club. She had been to proms at both Princeton and Yale. Her family had spent most of their summers visiting Uxbridge, Massachusetts, where her mother had grown up and where many of her mother's family still lived. Mary and her parents had also gone to a ranch in Montana, and she had been a guest of the Stevens family at a ranch in Wyoming. Mary went away to Miss Hall's, a boarding school in Pittsfield, Massachusetts, for grades ten and eleven, where she played field hockey. Subsequently she attended Miss Wheeler's, a boarding school in Providence, Rhode Island, for grades twelve and a postgraduate year. She had taken some French courses and was 5'6" tall.[3]

Both of Mary Warren's parents came from old New England families. Mary's father, Frank Dale Warren, had a father who had been born in Brighton, Massachusetts, and a mother who was from North Andover, Massachusetts. Because Frank's mother died in the process of childbirth, his maternal grandmother and her maiden sister had raised him in a large Victorian mansion known as Bellevue, situated on two hundred acres in North Andover, Massachusetts.

Mary's father, Frank Warren, graduated from Philips

Academy at Andover, Massachusetts, and then from Amherst College in 1883, where he was a member of the DKE fraternity. After college, he went into the paper business in Pepperell, Massachusetts, where he came to know William C. Clarke Jr., who asked Frank to join his business as a partner in their office at 225 Fifth Avenue in New York City. The firm of Clarke & Company was a wholesale manufacturer and distributor of paper. The commute for Frank from Plainfield, New Jersey, to his office in New York City was about two and a half hours each way, including a ride on the Staten Island Ferry. Frank usually worked for a half day on Saturdays, so Mary saw relatively little of her father while she was growing up. Mary had only one sibling—an older brother named Frank D. ("Dale") Warren Jr.[4]

Frank loved gardening and animals. He also liked antiques and "old things," including leather-bound books. In Fanwood, there was a man who slept upstairs in the barn. He drove the horses, helped feed the animals, and took care of the garden. There was also a maid who did the cooking. Frank enjoyed smoking a cigar and often played bridge while he was commuting on the train to New York City. Mary described her father as being a perfectionist who was a firm advocate of a classical education and the humanities. He stood out against progress, even to the extent of flaunting his attachment to horses and buggies for almost a decade after the invention of the automobile. Both of Mary's parents had been teetotalers, but they would enjoy a glass of Chianti in the evenings. Frank apparently got depressed whenever he lost money in the stock market.[5]

Frank's mother, Louise (Taft) Warren, had graduated

as the valedictorian of her high school class in Uxbridge, Massachusetts, and then attended Wellesley College for one year. During the summer after her freshman year at college, she took a job as a "companion and tutor" in Pepperell, Massachusetts, where she met her future husband. Louise's father had been county commissioner in Uxbridge and was a distant relative to US President William H. Taft (who came to visit Frank and Louise Warren in Plainfield in 1916, three years after he finished his term as president).[6]

When Frank and Louise Warren moved to Fanwood, New Jersey, two other couples joined them in the move there. One was John D. Stevens (later CEO of the textile company bearing his name) and his wife (John had been an usher in Frank and Louise Warren's wedding); the other was John Stevens's sister and her husband. At one time, Frank Warren served as the mayor of Fanwood, New Jersey—a town that had a population of about four hundred in those days. Then, in 1904, all three couples moved to Plainfield, New Jersey, for better schools. John Stevens's family was originally from North Andover, Massachusetts, where Frank had grown up.

Eric L. Hedstrom Sr.

Eric Sr. was born in Buffalo, New York, on March 12, 1899, the oldest of three children of Arthur and Katherine Hedstrom. He had grown up on the Four Winds Farm just outside of Buffalo, attended the Nichols School in Buffalo for four years, and then the Hill School, a boarding school in Pottstown, Pennsylvania, for two years.[7]

While at Yale, Eric Sr.—who had the nickname of

"Rick" at college—was a member of the Wolf's Head Senior Society and of the DKE fraternity. His involvement with the US Navy started when he joined the Yale Officer's Naval Training Unit, which lasted for most of his freshman year. Then, during the summer between freshman and sophomore years, he went to a "Summer Training Unit in Madison, Connecticut." Although he was qualified to be an ensign, he was unable to be commissioned because he was underage. Finally, he was enlisted in September 1918 and saw active duty on the USS *Pelican* minesweeper and on submarine chaser #295 in the Sixth Naval District in Charleston, South Carolina.[8] However, Eric Sr. was very fortunate since WWI was effectively ended when Germany signed the Armistice on November 11, 1918.[9] He received his honorable discharge in May 1919. Therefore, from the time when he enlisted until the time the war ended was only a little more than two months.

Eric Sr. was an attractive young man and an unusually gifted athlete. At Yale, he had played on the varsity tennis team in 1920 and the university's squash team in 1919 and 1920. He had won the freshman singles tennis tournament and was a runner-up in the university's doubles tennis tournament. He was also quite good at golf, although he was never able to beat his father in that sport. Eric Sr. graduated from Yale with a BA degree. He was six feet tall.[10]

Eric Sr. and Mary Settle in Buffalo

After their wedding and a honeymoon in Seal Harbor, Maine, Eric Sr. and Mary moved into the house of Arthur and Katherine Hedstrom for the summer while the gatehouse at the entrance to the Four Winds Farm property was being made ready for them. Eric Sr. was then twenty-two, and Mary was twenty-one. They lived in the gatehouse for about three years.[11] Shortly after they were married, Mary's parents—Frank and Louise Warren—came to visit at the Four Winds Farm. In a letter to his son, Frank Warren wrote that "This [Four Winds Farm] is certainly a most beautiful place and so comfortable. Eric and Mary have such a dear little home [the gatehouse]. I have been to the [Tennis and Squash] Club to see Eric play squash. They have a very fine club with both tennis and squash courts."[12]

Eric Sr.'s mother, Katherine Hedstrom, had insisted on decorating the gatehouse for Eric Sr. and Mary as a wedding present. She also provided them with a maid, although Mary didn't really want one at the time. During those years, Eric Sr. and Mary were expected to join Arthur and Katherine Hedstrom for either lunch or dinner on Thursdays and Sundays.[13]

On June 2, 1922, Eric Jr. was born while they were living in the gatehouse. Mary joined the YWCA Board and served as their treasurer. She was also involved with the Girls Clubs of Buffalo and many social activities, including the Junior League. Both Eric Sr. and Mary joined Arthur and Katherine Hedstrom in being Prohibitionists, although this was quite an unpopular position to take in those days.[14]

Eric Sr. and Mary attended the First Presbyterian Church at Symphony Circle in Buffalo. Mary's parents were both originally Unitarians, but in Plainfield, New Jersey, the family decided to attend the Crescent Avenue Presbyterian Church, so at that time, Mary felt that she was a Presbyterian.[15]

During the 1920s, Eric Sr. spent quite a bit of time playing polo at the Buffalo Country Club. His mother had bought four polo ponies for him and paid for a groom. Given that Eric Sr. was such a gifted athlete, he eventually became a three-goal polo player. (His father, Arthur, had gotten to be a two-goal player.) The ratings run from minus two to plus ten. For example, in the UK, only about 3 percent of the 1,500 rated polo players were at the level of three-goal or higher in 1993.[16] One of the top polo players in the US (with a seven-goal rating) was also a good friend of Eric Sr.'s—Seymour H. Knox Jr., a diminutive man known to close friends as "Shorty." He had attended the Nichols School in Buffalo and was in the Yale class of 1920—one year behind Eric Sr. Seymour Knox Jr. was an usher in the wedding of Eric Sr. and also played with him on the Yale University squash team.

Eric Sr. kept playing tennis and squash in Buffalo at the Tennis and Squash Club. He wrote two articles for magazines, the first on the game of tennis, "Doubles Position Play and Strategy" in August 1937, and the other article on the game of squash, "More Emphasis on Shot Making" in 1952.[17]

Meanwhile, in about 1923, Arthur Hedstrom purchased the Cooper Paper Box Company, a manufacturer of folding boxes used by companies such as Philip Morris, Colgate Palmolive, and Bayer. The company had been started in 1881. When he initially joined Cooper in 1923, Eric Sr. had the title of vice president. Then in 1927, he became president and general manager. During WWI, the Cooper Paper Box Company "operated as a defense plant." His father, Arthur, gave Eric Sr. enough of the common stock so that he had 51 percent of the outstanding common stock at that time. His salary and the common dividends provided him with a nice income. In effect, Arthur had purchased Cooper for his son Eric Sr. to run once he had graduated from Yale and gotten married. Eric Sr. never ran the coal business because after the merger with the Spaulding family in 1927, it was agreed that one of the Spauldings would manage the combined company.[18]

Eric Sr. took on various business roles that were related to his father—director of the Hedstrom-Spalding Coal Company for fifteen years, director of the Hedstrom-Spalding Trucking Company for fifteen years, director of the E. L. Hedstrom Coal Company for ten years (and treasurer for three years), and treasurer of the Hedstrom Holding Company for fifteen years. He was also "a director of a local bank, director of an investment trust company and two other industrial firms," according to his notes.[19]

Eric Sr. followed his father's footsteps in contributing and giving back to the Buffalo community. He was president of the Boys Clubs of Buffalo for fifteen years and was a director of the Buffalo Association for the Blind.[20]

In 1924, Eric Sr. and Mary started to build their home at 32 St. Catherine's Court in Buffalo. Their daughter, Sonja, was born on March 2 of that year. When they moved in to their new house, they had a cook, a waitress, and a nurse. Mary said later that she spent quite a bit of time writing out menus for the meals for her family and the staff. She also said that the stock market "crash came in 1929 and luckily, we had spent our money on the house or we would have lost it in the stock market." In 1931, Eric Sr. and Mary went to Italy and France for a tenth-anniversary holiday that was paid for by Katherine Hedstrom.[21]

In 1925, Mary's father died, and she went to spend some time with her mother. In those days, Mary's parents usually rented a house for the summer in Cohasset, Massachusetts, or in Madison, Connecticut. Mary's mother was diagnosed with cancer in 1934, and she passed away in 1935. Mary then went to Plainfield to settle her mother's estate, staying with Aunt Edna Stevens, Bob Stevens's mother.[22]

Eric Sr. and Mary's Divorce

In 1938, Eric Sr. asked Mary (who were then ages thirty-nine and thirty-eight, respectively) for a divorce, so Mary went to Reno, Nevada, for six weeks to obtain the divorce, as it was quite uncommon in those days.[23] Eric Sr. then changed his mind and asked Mary to get back together, but she said no. Eric Sr.'s reason for requesting a divorce was not because there was another woman in his life; it was that he was not well—"mixed up" and depressed.

In 1939, Mary moved into her own apartment at 33 Oakland Place in Buffalo; Eric Sr. moved into an apartment at 13 Mayfair Lane in Buffalo; Eric Jr. went off to Pomfret, a boarding school in Pomfret, Connecticut, and Sonja went off to Garrison Forest, a boarding school near Baltimore, Maryland.[24]

Eric Sr.: 1938–1951

During the thirteen-year period from when Eric Sr. and Mary were divorced in 1938 until Eric Sr. was remarried to his second wife in 1951, Eric Sr. went through a very difficult time. In addition to being deeply affected by his divorce, he also had some problems that became evident about seven years prior to the divorce—problems that related to his upbringing. During these years, Eric Sr. continued to have the responsibilities of managing the Cooper Paper Box Company, as its president and general manager. His father, Arthur, passed away in 1946, and his mother passed away in 1952. Arthur had made Eric Sr. a trustee of his trust.[25]

Mary after 1938

After the divorce, Mary lived at 33 Oakland Place until she moved to Boston, Massachusetts. During this time, Mary took her two children to a ranch in Montana for several summer holidays. She was fortunate to have inherited quite a bit of money from her parents, so in 1942, she moved into an apartment at 90 Commonwealth Avenue in Boston, along with a cook. That same year, her daughter, Sonja, had her coming-out party. Mary was a volunteer—"almost full-time"—at the Red Cross. She also enjoyed going to the symphony at Boston's Symphony Hall, and she joined the Children's Aid Society. Her daughter, Sonja, was then living in Boston, so she took a nurse's aide course and worked at Massachusetts General Hospital.[26]

Mary's older brother, Dale Warren, had gone to Philips Academy in Andover, Massachusetts, and graduated from Princeton University in 1919 and then from Columbia University with a master of arts in sociology. He had also been in the US Naval Reserve for nine months. He spent his career as an editor of Houghton Mifflin in Boston. He loved the opera and took an annual vacation to Bermuda for many years. Dale remained a bachelor for his whole life, as he had a broken love affair when he was younger. He lived at the Ritz Carlton Hotel in Boston during the week and had a weekend house in Scituate, Massachusetts, where he was near his sister, Mary. On the weekends, Dale Warren would usually go over to his sister, Mary's, house for Sunday lunch. Dale passed away in 1978 at the age of eighty-one.[27]

In 1943, Sonja started taking a course in occupational therapy. Meanwhile, Eric Jr. had joined the Army Air Corps after completing three years at Yale. Then Mary became engaged to W. Clarke Atwater, the son of Jessie (Clarke) Atwater of Milton, Massachusetts, and the late Henry D. Atwater. They were married on February 12, 1944, in King's Chapel, a Unitarian church in downtown Boston. Clarke was then thirty-nine, and Mary was forty-four. Mary had met Clarke at a cocktail party that her brother, Dale Warren, had given at his weekend house in North Pembroke, Massachusetts (where he spent weekends before moving to Scituate, Massachusetts). Clarke's uncle, William Clarke Jr., and Mary's father had been business partners in New York City. In fact, Clarke's maternal grandfather, William Clarke Sr., had founded the company. Clarke had gone to Middlesex School in Concord, Massachusetts, and graduated from Harvard in 1928. At Harvard, he was the president of the Glee Club. He had been stricken with polio at the age of five, so Middlesex taught him how to row crew and how to sing—two activities at which he could excel without being held back by his polio. Mary then purchased a colonial house on fifty acres at 473 River Street in Norwell, Massachusetts, about twenty-five miles southeast of Boston, where she and Clarke settled. In later years, Mary said that in politics, she was a registered Republican but didn't feel that Ronald Reagan was sufficiently concerned about poor people.[28]

On July 14, 1945, Sonja was married to Carlton P. Cooke Jr. of Buffalo. Then, in 1950, Eric Jr. was married to Eloise G. Herrick of Buffalo. Mary Atwater took a holiday in Bermuda in the springtime for many years. Her children and their families would usually drive from Buffalo to Boston to visit Mary and Clarke in Norwell in the summers. Clarke Atwater had purchased the Cohasset Lumber Company with a friend, which provided him with a steady job for about ten years. Then he became a residential real estate broker.[29]

In 1961, Mary and Clarke decided to move into a smaller house that required much less maintenance, just down the street at 138 River Street in Norwell. She and Clarke lived there until Clarke passed away in 1984 at the age of seventy-nine. At that time, Mary decided to move back to Buffalo, New York, to be closer to her two children and her five grandchildren. Mary passed away on June 7, 1997, in Buffalo at the age of ninety-seven.[30] Her daughter Sonja passed away in 2004.[31]

Cooper Paper Box: 1927–1956

Eric Sr. was president and general manager of the Cooper Paper Box Company from 1927 until 1956. For about nineteen years prior to 1952, Cooper did not lose money, even during the Depression. The company's offices were at 368 Sycamore Street in Buffalo for most of those years. It had annual sales of approximately $1 million toward the end of that period, a level of sales that was similar to the E. L. Hedstrom Coal Company. The company's average profits during this period were about $55,000 annually. Cooper had been producing about ten thousand folding boxes a day—boxes that were being sold throughout the US and even to South Africa.[32]

In 1945, after WWII had ended and after he had graduated from Yale, Eric Jr. moved back to Buffalo to live with his father. Eric Sr. had encouraged his son to join the Cooper Paper Box Company, and Eric Jr. thought that he would "give it a try," although he had wanted to go to the Harvard Business School at that time. Eric Jr. became a vice president and treasurer of Cooper.[33]

In 1952, the Hedstrom family made two relatively big decisions—first to invest about $175,000 in a "rotogravure printing press" and related equipment (e.g., an automatic gluing machine, a new loading dock). Second, they reached out to friends to raise an additional amount of money, including the families of two of Eric Jr.'s close friends— Carlton P. ("Carl") Cooke Jr. and Murray Warner. Carl became assistant treasurer, and Murray became assistant secretary of Cooper. The plan was to invest in the upgraded equipment to provide for a new business opportunity for Eric Jr., Carl, and Murray—all recent college graduates. The idea was that the larger printing press would enable the company to solicit larger national accounts.[34]

By the early 1950s, Cooper's capital structure was reasonably complicated for a company of that size; Cooper had common and preferred stock, various types of secured bank loans, equipment loans, and several types of debentures. The company's ownership was also complicated by the different interests of many shareholders, most of whom were members of the Hedstrom family and their friends. The new rotogravure press didn't fit in the company's office space at the Sycamore plant, so it was located nearby at 19 Harwood Place. At that time, the warehouse facility and finished goods inventory were maintained at 465 Eagle Street. In January 1957, the company's offices were relocated to 19 Harwood Place, where its operations were consolidated.[35]

Unfortunately, the additional investment in Cooper did not work out as everyone had hoped. The new printing press increased the company's capacity from about ten thousand paper boxes per day to about sixty-five thousand boxes per hour. The rotogravure press would take paperboard from a roll, print the boxes with a five-color printing process, die-cut them, and produce the folding boxes.[36]

From 1952 until 1955, Cooper lost money. The costs of implementing the new printing press had been underestimated, and the company didn't generate the additional sales that would have been needed to keep the new printing press fully utilized.[37]

At a meeting of Cooper's board of directors on January 20, 1956, Eric Jr. was made the company's president and general manager. Carl became treasurer, and Murray became secretary. As of that date, the new generation took over responsibility for the company's management.[38]

Eric Sr.'s Marriage to Cecil

On April 30, 1951, in the Sixth Presbyterian Church in Washington, DC, Eric Sr. was married to Cecil Elaine Eustace Smith of Toronto, Canada.[39] Cecil was the daughter of Mr. and Mrs. Eustace Smith of Toronto. She was a champion figure skater who had competed twice in the winter Olympics (1924 and 1928) and who had won a silver medal in the 1930 World Figure Skating Championships. Cecil's mother had won the 1892 Canadian Tennis Championship, and her father ran a distillery in Toronto.[40]

Initially, Eric Sr. and Cecil made their home at 200 Summer Street in Buffalo. Then they purchased a house and property on North Davis Road in East Aurora, New York, that had been owned by Alfred H. Schoellkopf. However, before long, this marriage stopped working out, and the two were separated. One family member mentioned that Cecil had two sisters who had both married wealthy men.

Eric Sr. then moved to Vero Beach, Florida, and went through another very bad time in his life. Apparently, he was on the phone with his mother on a daily basis during that time. When he went to stay with her in Buffalo, she would arrange for two nurses to take care of him.[41]

Due to Eric Sr.'s troubles, his sister Brenda and his brother Lars asked the court in Florida to have him removed from his role as the trustee on their father's trust. In January 1956, the court in Florida determined that Eric Sr. was not competent enough to manage his own affairs, and two months later, he was removed as trustee of the Arthur Hedstrom Trust.[42] Then, at the same meeting of the Cooper Paper Box Board of Directors that installed Eric Jr. as president and general manager, Eric Sr. was removed from having that same title.[43]

Eric Sr.'s Marriage to Ethel

After getting legally separated from Cecil and losing his two sources of income (his salary from Cooper and his trustee fee), Eric Sr. decided to get together with Ethel (Hoyt) Peale of Darien, Connecticut. At that time, Ethel was the widow of Dr. Franklin V. Peale. Ethel's parents were John Sherman Hoyt and Ethel Phelps (Stokes) Hoyt of Darien. Ethel's father had at one time owned all of what is now Contentment Island in Darien, some of the most beautiful waterfront property in that part of Connecticut.[44] Ethel had a house on Contentment Island overlooking Long Island Sound. Eric Sr. had met Ethel through friends from Buffalo who knew both of them.[45] Ethel was warned at that time that Eric Sr. had two broken marriages and had at one time apparently had a drinking problem, but Ethel wouldn't even listen to this advice, as she had fallen completely in love with Eric Sr.

Eric Sr. and Ethel were married on July 15, 1957, in the Church-by-the-Sea, a Presbyterian church in Ft. Lauderdale, Florida.[46] They spent one of their holidays cruising among the islands in the Bahamas. The three and a half years that Eric Sr. and Ethel were married were probably the happiest of Eric Sr.'s life.

Eric Sr. died on February 14, 1961 (at age sixty-one) of a heart attack in Bangkok, Thailand, while he and Ethel were there on a vacation.[47]

Looking Back

The life of Eric Sr. was filled with some fabulous highs and some horrible lows. He was a very attractive man and an unusually gifted athlete whose accomplishments in polo, tennis, squash, and golf were nothing short of spectacular. Two of his wives—the first and third (Mary and Ethel)—were both well known by his family. They were both unusually nice and wonderful women. His first wife, Mary, was in particular a beautiful person in so many ways. Eric Sr. and Mary raised two children who went on to lead quite successful lives, with children of their own. They had given each of their children a very high-quality education.

Why did it all go so wrong? His son, Eric Jr., said of his father: "He had so much—good looks, good athlete, good mind—but he had been very, very spoiled by his mother and he had been effectively insulated from life's school of hard knocks. He never invested any money in Cooper beyond what he absolutely had to invest to keep the company going—partly because he had lived through the depression and wanted to be able to lock it up and walk away if he had to do that. The result was that Cooper was starved of the investment that would have been needed to keep it a strong company. Eric Sr. enjoyed being an investor in the stock market and he was good at employee relations but he was not a builder. He lacked self-confidence and was not very comfortable with his peers."

Ethel, Eric Sr.'s third wife, wrote to Eric Jr. after his father had passed away, saying, "I thank God continually for such a sudden, peaceful and happy ending to a life filled with so much unhappiness. I have such mixed feelings—why such a thing should happen just when everything had nearly straightened out and your father was his old self again. He had many fine qualities but for some unknown reason, he never seemed able to project his true self towards others the way he wanted so awfully to do. He seemed so confident and strong, whereas really, he was insecure and in need of constant building up and confidence; this went way, way back. I have had great joy in knowing and seeing him enjoy life—maybe not to the full but certainly more than he had for quite a while. I have gained greatly from knowing and loving him—only wish it could have been longer."

Mary (Warren) Hedstrom, Eric Sr.'s first wife, said, "It was hard as a young bride moving into a home that had been completely furnished by my mother-in-law, and hard to be expected to have lunch or dinner with my in-laws twice-a-week. When Eric Sr. started playing polo, he got himself into a group of very wealthy people with whom he couldn't keep up."

The truth is that perhaps it all started when Eric Sr. was a very little boy. His parents, Arthur and Katherine, decided to leave him and go on a vacation to the Grand Canyon and Mexico when Eric Sr. was only about one year old. Then, for the next three years, when Eric Sr. was a tiny baby, his parents were thoroughly engaged with their socializing in the South of France.

Brenda Hedstrom's second husband, who was a successful businessman, completed an analysis of what happened to the Cooper Paper Box Company and why it lost money. He concluded that the fateful decision to purchase the rotogravure printing press was either an unwise investment decision or the execution of this decision did not have the appropriate management controls to ensure that it was implemented successfully. Apparently, Eric Sr. ran Cooper as a one-man show and didn't have anyone who could challenge him on various business decisions. For example, if the company's board had some strong independent outside directors, they might have required the company to have stronger internal controls, budgets, and sales forecasts, as well as programs for achieving the company's objectives.

By the time Eric Sr. was pushed out as president, the company was highly leveraged with bank loans that were secured by warehouse receipts, accounts receivable, inventory, and almost all other assets. However, one has to ask how much of this was the fault of Eric Sr. since he was put into the job of managing a company when he was right out of college, with essentially no prior business experience that would have prepared him for such a position.

In looking at the complete picture, one has to look at the two children and five grandchildren of Eric Sr. Without a doubt, much of the credit for how they all turned out goes to his wife, Mary. Eric Sr.'s offspring would all agree with that assessment.

Photographs for Chapter Four

Frank Dale Warren (Mary's father)

Louise Taft Warren (Mary's mother)

Eric Sr.—second from right—playing polo.

Eric Sr.

Mary (Warren) Hedstrom

Frank D. ("Dale") Warren Jr.

Clarke and Mary Atwater in Bermuda.

Cecil Hedstrom (on right), second wife of Eric Sr.

Ethel (Hoyt Peale) Hedstrom and Eric Sr. She was his third wife.

View of Ethel Hedstrom's house on Contentment Island in Darien, Connecticut.

Chapter Five

ERIC L. HEDSTROM JR.
(1922–2014)

The self-effacing person is soothing and
gracious ... Humility is freedom from the need
to prove you are superior all the time ... egotism
is ... self-concerned, competitive, and distinction-
hungry. Humility is infused with lovely emotions
like admiration, companionship, and gratitude.

DAVID BROOKS (1961–)

Eric Leonard
Hedstrom, Jr.
("Eric Jr.")

L e Mirador Hotel sits on the side of Mont-Pelerin just
above the town of Vevey, Switzerland. One of the
many reasons why this hotel enjoys a five-star rating is
because the panoramic view from the hotel out across Lake
Geneva toward the Swiss and French Alps is truly one of the
most spectacular views anywhere in the world.

In 1976, Eric L. Hedstrom Jr. held a business conference
at this hotel. He had invited the general managers of each
of Graphic Controls Corporation's international subsidiaries
and also their wives for a several-day conference. The couples
began arriving—from England, France, Belgium, Spain,
Canada, Australia, Mexico, Brazil, Venezuela, and India.

While the men were in their meetings (in those days, sadly, there were no women general managers), Eric Jr.'s wife, Suzie Hedstrom, took the wives on various day trips—for example, to see the picturesque little town of Gruyere that is famous for its cheese.

The Graphic Controls Corporation ("Graphic") had acquired the Cooper Paper Box Company ("Cooper") in April 1959. In November 1960, Eric Jr. had been named director of a new market research division at Graphic. In February 1965, Eric Jr. was named manager of export sales and head of the new International Operations Department of Graphic. This position evolved into the general manager of the company's international division. In December 1970, Eric Jr. was elected to the office of secretary of the company.[1]

Eric Jr.'s Early Years

Eric L. Hedstrom Jr. was born on June 2, 1922, in Buffalo, New York, the oldest of two children of Eric Sr. and Mary (Warren) Hedstrom.[2] His first few years were spent in the gatehouse at the Four Winds Farm of his paternal grandparents. Then when he was about three years old, his parents moved into their new house at 32 St. Catherine's Court in Buffalo. Eric Jr. attended the Elmwood School and then, starting with the sixth grade, the Nichols School in Buffalo. For several summers, he went to the Winona Camp in Bridgton, Maine. His mother had gone to the nearby summer camp for girls called Wyonegonic when she was young.[3]

In 1938, Eric Jr. learned that his parents were getting a divorce. He was sixteen at the time. He later said, "This came as a shock and complete surprise for me." After spending a month on a ranch in Montana with his mother and sister, he started attending the Pomfret School, a boarding school in Pomfret, Connecticut. In 1941, Eric Jr. started at Yale, and that November, he learned of the Japanese attack on Pearl Harbor. He managed to complete three academic years in chemical engineering at Yale before being called to service in November 1943.[4]

After basic training in North Carolina, Eric Jr. went back to Yale for five months before receiving his second lieutenant commission in June 1944. He then went for training in Colorado, Mississippi, and Texas. Later in 1944, Eric Jr. departed from Seattle for Hawaii, where he received training for the invasion of Okinawa, Japan. At that time, he was promoted to first lieutenant.[5]

Eric Jr. arrived in Okinawa on April 30 as an aircraft maintenance officer with the 163rd Liaison Squadron of the Seventh Air Force. The Battle of Okinawa had begun thirty days earlier, on April 1. He witnessed bombing attacks by the kamikaze planes almost each evening. His role was to set up forty new L-5 planes that had each arrived in large wooden crates on a runway in central Okinawa. These planes, which were small (like a modern-day piper cub), did reconnaissance work and then transported wounded soldiers back from forward areas. Eric Jr. and his colleagues managed to set up thirty of these planes. Interestingly, once each plane was assembled, the crew would take Eric Jr. or one of his colleagues up for the first test flight to be sure the plane was in good working condition. He lived in underground shelters until Okinawa was declared secured on June 22, 1944.[6]

In the latter part of 1944, Eric Jr. was sent back to Pearl Harbor to supervise the construction of auxiliary gas tanks that were to permit the planes to fly all the way to Kyushu, Japan, for the planned invasion. He later wrote, "Fortunately, the first atom bomb was dropped on Hiroshima [August 6, 1945] while I was in Pearl Harbor." Although WWII ended on September 2, 1945, he was sent back to Okinawa for another year. He said that the reason for this was because he didn't have enough time in service to have priority in going home. In August 1946, he returned to San Francisco by ship. He was promoted to captain in September 1946 and received his honorable discharge.[7] The related papers noted his height as being 5'8".[8] The three-month Battle of Okinawa was the last major battle of WWII. There had been 545,000 Americans involved in the battle, of whom 12,520 died. The Japanese had 94,136 fatalities during that battle, and about one quarter of the island's prewar local population also died.[9]

Eric Jr. then returned to Yale to complete his final year, graduating with a bachelor of engineering degree in June 1947. He didn't join the Wolf's Head Senior Society, where his father had been a member, as it was not possible for engineering students. In the later part of 1947, Eric Jr. moved in with his father in the apartment on Mayfair Lane in Buffalo and started work at the Cooper Paper Box Company.[10]

Eric Jr. was a gifted athlete, like his father and grandfather. He played soccer at Yale, where he felt he could have made their varsity team, but he didn't want to make the time commitment of playing in both the fall and the spring. He played on the five-person squash team for the Buffalo Tennis and Squash Club that went to the Nationals in two different years—one in Boston and the other in Philadelphia. Eric Jr. also enjoyed playing golf throughout most of his life.[11]

Eric Jr. Is Married

In June 1949, Eric Jr. wrote to his mother informing her that he planned to get married to Eloise ("Suzie") Gilbert Herrick. He said, "I am supremely happy and so much in love with Suzie."[12] The engagement was announced in September 1949.[13] He and Suzie were then married in Trinity Episcopal Church in Buffalo on January 7, 1950. Eric Jr. was then twenty-seven, and Suzie was twenty. The two of them went to Jamaica for their honeymoon. When they returned, they moved into an apartment at 788 West Ferry Street in Buffalo.[14]

Suzie Hedstrom was the youngest of three children of Sherlock ("Shirts") A. Herrick Sr. and Eloise ("Bobby") G. Stockton. Shirts had been born the oldest of three children of Frank Rufus Herrick and Josephine Pomeroy. He was raised in Cleveland, Ohio, where his father was an attorney. His mother, Josephine, was the daughter of Theodore M. Pomeroy, who had served as the Speaker of the US House of Representatives. Theodore Pomeroy had been elected as a Republican representative from Auburn, New York, in 1860, the same year that Abe Lincoln was elected president. Both Shirts and his father, Frank, had graduated from Yale. Shirts was a member of Yale's class of 1919 and a member of Wolf's Head senior society at Yale. Frank went on to attend the Harvard Law School.[15]

Bobby (Stockton) Herrick had grown up in Buffalo. Her

father, Lewis Stockton, was an attorney. Her mother, Eloise Gilbert, was originally from Baltimore, Maryland. Both Bobby and Shirts were Episcopalians.

Suzie Hedstrom had grown up in Buffalo, where she attended the Elmwood-Franklin School and the Buffalo Seminary School. After graduating from the Buffalo Seminary, she spent a postgraduate year at the Chateaux Mont Choisi, a boarding school in Lausanne, Switzerland, where she improved her French and took piano lessons.[16]

On April 14, 1951, Eric Jr. and Suzie's first son, Mitchell, was born. Then, in 1952, they moved out to East Aurora, New York, a small town about twenty miles southeast of Buffalo. They had found a little (six hundred square feet) house to rent on Girdle Road there. They had chosen this town because in 1926, Suzie Hedstrom's parents had purchased about one hundred acres of land across from the East Aurora Country Club in East Aurora. They had been on a weekend cross-country skiing trip to that town along with other friends from Buffalo when they discovered the property. Over the course of the next fifty-plus years, Suzie's parents would transform this property (which the family referred to as "the Farm") into a beautiful family compound with a lake, a pond, fields, woods, a cabin, and a boathouse. Initially, Suzie's parents used this house (which they called the 'boathouse') as a weekend home while maintaining their apartment in Buffalo.[17]

In 1954, Eric Jr. and Suzie decided to purchase land overlooking this lake on the family Farm ("for $1 and a lot of love"), where they designed and built their own house. Suzie's brother and his wife—Sherlock ("Skip") A. Herrick Jr. and Joy Herrick—obtained land from Sherlock Sr. on the other side of the lake, where they built their own house.[18]

On September 1, 1953, Eric Jr and Suzie's second son, Gilbert, was born, and on December 8, 1954, their third son, Roger, was born. During these years, Eric Jr. took courses in American Federal Government and the Evolution of Music at the University of Buffalo as well as a course to become certified with the National Association of Cost Accountants.[19] Several years earlier, he had taught himself how to play Handel's Largo on the piano.

Eric Jr.'s Career at Cooper Paper Box

In 1952, the Hedstrom family was joined by the families of Carl Cooke and Murray Warner in contributing additional capital to Cooper in order for the company to purchase a new rotogravure printing press and other capital improvements. Carl Cooke and Murray Warner joined Cooper at that time.[20]

One week after Carl and Murray joined Cooper, Eric Jr. became ill with polio. He spent six weeks in the hospital and six months recovering in the Buffalo apartment of Suzie's parents at 40 Ashland Avenue in Buffalo. Then he began daily therapy at the Sister Elizabeth Kenny Foundation, using crutches and a leg brace—the latter for about two years. Jonas Salk didn't invent the polio vaccine until January 1953.[21]

Meanwhile, the overall situation at Cooper continued to deteriorate, as mentioned earlier, since the costs of implementing the new rotogravure press had been underestimated. Complicating things was the fact that Eric Jr.'s father was still the president and general manager. In addition, Eric Sr. and his brother and sister were still large shareholders, so when the losses continued throughout the 1950s, they all became anxious to sell the business.[22]

In June 1953, Eric Jr. returned to work after recuperating from polio. Once Eric Jr. became president and general manager of Cooper on January 20, 1956, replacing his father in that role, his largest shareholders strongly urged him to sell Cooper as quickly as possible. At that time, Cooper was losing about $20,000 a month. Within a few months, Eric Jr. engaged C. Lester Horn, a consultant in New York, New York, to find a buyer for Cooper.[23]

In February 1959, Eric Jr. received a letter of intent from Max Clarkson, president of Graphic Controls, expressing a willingness to recommend to his board an offer of approximately $255,000, provided that the three individuals active in the management of Cooper (Eric Jr., Carl, and Murray) would take stock in Graphic Controls as part of the transaction.[24] A few years later, Graphic was the world's leading chart manufacturer that supplied 85 percent of Fortune's 500 largest corporations. By 1976, Graphic had annual revenues of about $60 million.[25]

In explaining this offer in a letter to family members, Eric Jr. said, "Though this deal may not appear unduly good, we must remember that Cooper has been riding on the rim of bankruptcy for the last three years and the future does not look any brighter. We are in no bargaining position whatsoever."[26] The acquisition of Cooper by Graphic Controls was completed in April 1959. Eric Jr. then joined Graphic Controls as a full-time employee.

Eric Jr.'s Life on the Farm

For the three children of Eric Jr. and Suzie, growing up on the Farm was an idealistic childhood. Skip and Joy Herrick had three children, so there was lots of family around— grandparents, aunts and uncles, and cousins. Occasionally, the family of Skip and Suzie's sister, Patricia, would come to visit from their home in Cleveland, Ohio. The cousins built tree houses in the woods together, rode a go-cart and a mini-bike, and found an endless number of activities to keep them all busy.

There were two special holidays that all of the family members usually celebrated together: the Fourth of July and Thanksgiving. For the former, there was a parade with everyone walking, dressed in funny outfits for the occasion, from Skip and Joy's house, past the boathouse, to the Hedstroms' house, with refreshments at the end.

There was an unusually strong element of patriotism that was in the air during this occasion, given the military service of three members of the family. Shirts Herrick had served in WWI in the Battles of the Meuse-Argonne near Verdun, France, and then in WWII he had participated in the landings in North Africa and Italy. He had eventually achieved the rank of major in the US Army. Skip Herrick had participated in the D-Day landings on Omaha Beach in northern France, while Eric Jr. had fought in the Battle of Okinawa in the Pacific theater. The second occasion, the Thanksgiving holiday, would usually begin with cocktails at the boathouse of Shirts and Bobby near the lake, then a beautiful Thanksgiving meal at the house of Skip and Joy, and finally dessert at the Hedstroms'.

Eric Jr., Suzie, and their children attended the St. Matthias Episcopal Church in East Aurora almost every Sunday. In 1984, Eric Jr. and Suzie built a tennis court on their property and hosted an annual tennis tournament for nearby friends and family. They referred to these tournaments as "Wimblestrom." There were awards and many enjoyable moments. Eric Jr. also joined one of the local country clubs, where he played golf in a foursome on most Sunday mornings. In 1994, Suzie's mother passed away at the age of ninety-two. Her father, Shirts, had passed away in 1971 at the age of seventy-four.[27]

Piano Concerts

Bobby Herrick was quite an accomplished pianist. She had two Steinway pianos in her apartment at 40 Ashland Avenue in Buffalo, where she and her husband lived during the week before they made their permanent home in East Aurora. She played regularly with a few friends and taught piano to students during the Depression.

Bobby's daughter, Suzie Hedstrom, was also an accomplished pianist. One event that brought the mother and daughter much closer together was when the cabin that had been located in the woods on the Farm was moved next to the boathouse and the two Steinway pianos were brought out from Buffalo and placed in the cabin (which was then renamed the Piano Studio). For eleven years, from 1964 until 1974, Bobby and Suzie joined with two other local women piano players (Joy DesGeorges and Roseanne Gillogly) to play "eight hands, two pianos." They gave an annual concert in the summer that was certainly one of the biggest highlights of the family's life on the Farm.

The programs included the piano music of Bach, Beethoven, Brahms, Chopin, Grieg, Handel, Mozart, Schubert, Schumann, Shostakovich, Sibelius, and Strauss as well as various other composers. The guests for these concerts were many family friends, including several friends from Buffalo that Bobby and Suzie had known socially there. The grandchildren were all put to work—parking cars, bartending, passing hors d'oeuvres, and generally being helpful. The guests sat just outside of the piano studio, under the trees. The doors and windows of the Piano Studio were all wide open, and the piano music poured out. It was all a magical, unforgettable experience to behold. For Suzie Hedstrom, these concerts were the high point of her life.

Suzie Hedstrom had a lifelong interest in classical music. She studied the piano for many years, completing five levels of "Piano Musicianship and Pedagogy" by Robert Pace. She also taught elementary piano students for twenty-four years from her home.

Eric Jr.'s Community Involvement

There were many ways that Eric Jr. gave back to his community. He served as a warden of the St. Matthias Episcopal Church in East Aurora; president, Episcopal Community Services; president, director, and chairman of Boys and Girls Clubs of Buffalo, Erie County, New York; vice chairman, United Way of Buffalo and Erie County; vice president, Western New York Grantmakers Association; chairman, Strategic Planning Advisory Committee, Erie Community College; director and vice president, United Health Foundation of Western New York; director and president, Sister Elizabeth Kenny Foundation of Western New York; a member of the board of trustees of Hospice of Southwest Florida; and director and vice president, Plantation Community Foundation, Venice, Florida.[28]

In politics, Eric Jr. and Suzie were moderate Republicans. On several occasions, Eric Jr. said that he had voted for a Democratic presidential candidate when he thought that person was better qualified.

Eric Jr. and Suzie's Travel

Since Eric Jr. was head of Graphic's International Group, with ten subsidiaries in various parts of the world, he spent a considerable amount of time traveling abroad. He kept a one-page summary of all the international trips that he had taken over the years. He was very meticulous and systematic about such things, perhaps due to his engineering background. In total, he figured that he had taken eighty-six international trips that were directly related to his job at Graphic. The number of visits that he made to specific countries (with several country visits common for each trip) were as follows: Belgium (twenty), France (fifty-two), Germany (twenty-seven), Spain (twenty-nine), the UK (thirty-four), Iran (three), Lebanon (two), India (seven), Japan (four), Hong Kong (four), Australia (three), Venezuela (nineteen), Brazil (seventeen), Mexico (thirteen), and many other countries for one or more visits each. Such a list of places visited does not capture the full depth of what he did when he arrived at many of these places. For the countries where Graphic had subsidiaries, he had the full range of management issues to contend with, including a review of their financial performance.[29]

There was one particular European trip that was quite different from all the others. The French subsidiary had been having some difficulties, so Eric Jr. was asked to spend about two months living near that subsidiary in the spring of 1978 to help try to turn the situation around. It was located in the town of Brie-Comte-Robert, about twenty miles southeast of Paris. His wife, Suzie, went along for that trip and acted as his secretary during their time there.

In addition to all of this international travel that was directly business related, he and his wife also took the following trips abroad, often with a group from the Buffalo Art Gallery or Yale University: the Mediterranean; Northern Italy and Southern France; Switzerland, Germany, and Austria; the Danube, Adriatic, and Budapest; the Caribbean; the Black Sea and Yalta; Spain, Morocco, and the Canary Islands; the Canadian Rockies; the Mississippi River on a paddleboat; the Panama Canal; and a Danube River cruise.[30]

In February 1978, Graphic was acquired by the Times Mirror Corporation, publisher of the *Los Angeles Times*. This provided a bit of a windfall for the Graphic shareholders.[31]

Eric Jr. and Suzie's Retirement

In December 1982, Eric Jr. retired from Graphic Controls. By the time he retired, the international operations of Graphic Controls had grown to $38 million in annual revenue. Eric Jr. did some consulting work for a few years, and then, in 1984, he was named president of America Works of New York, to run their Buffalo office. This was a for-profit firm that placed people who were on welfare into jobs. Under their contract with the state of New York, America Works was paid $3,500 each time they found a job for someone on welfare. During the two years that Eric Jr. worked there, he placed two hundred people into jobs who had previously been on welfare.[32]

In 1985, Eric Jr. and Suzie rented a house at the Plantation in Venice, Florida, for a month during the winter. After renting each winter for several years, they eventually purchased a house at the Plantation in 1988. By 1996, they sold their home in East Aurora, New York, and became full-time Florida residents.

In 2004, Eric Jr. and Suzie moved into a retirement community with some three hundred residential units called the Glenridge at the Palmer Ranch in Sarasota, Florida. The Glenridge had three types of residential units—houses, apartments for assisted living, and then skilled care. Suzie was diagnosed with macular degeneration in about 2000, and she could only see a little bit for her later years. In response to that, she started the Low Vision Group at the Glenridge to assist others who had similar difficulty with their eyesight. She also took her tape recorder and visited the skilled-care unit once a week to play music for the residents there, to cheer them up.

Eric Jr. passed away on June 14, 2014, at the age of ninety-two.[33] Suzie continued to live at the Glenridge, eventually moving into their skilled-care section for her last six months before she passed away on May 6, 2018, at the age of eighty-eight.[34]

Looking Back

Eric Jr. and Suzie were married for sixty-four years. They had many close friends in Buffalo and in Florida. By any reasonable measure, Eric Jr. had a very successful business career, managing to exit a very difficult situation with the family's Cooper Paper Box Company while he was still recovering from his polio and raising three very young boys at home, also managing to get himself a new promising career at Graphic Controls. His career at Graphic was successful, and perhaps more importantly, it was for him a very rewarding experience. This is partly a tribute to the Clarkson family, who owned Graphic and who made Eric Jr.'s career possible.

Raising three healthy sons within four years of one another in age, sending each of them to private school for their high school years, putting each of them through four years of college, and then watching each of them get married and have children of their own was certainly an achievement. Also, Eric Jr. and Suzie enjoyed about twenty-nine years of retirement in Florida where, at least in the earlier years, they both played a bit of golf and tennis. They got to know each of their six grandchildren—three boys and three girls.

Suzie Hedstrom was a regular attendee of the Sarasota Symphony Orchestra, which she loved. She also regularly attended the Anglican church that was just down the road from the Glenridge and a Bible study class that met twice a month at the Glenridge.

When Eric Jr. retired from Graphic, the manager of their UK subsidiary said, "He had a quiet and unassuming presence. He was a thoughtful and sensitive guy. He was a very patient and gentle person. He worked hard and was empathetic to the differences in various nationalities. This was very much appreciated by his business associates and is not a common trait among Americans. He was a very genuine person. He never sought the limelight. He was a kind and caring person—a real gentleman."

In Eric Jr.'s notes for what he might want for his memorial service, he asked that in addition to one or two hymns, he would like the guests to sing "America the Beautiful," a wish that was fulfilled.

Eric Jr.'s wife, Suzie, mentioned that her favorite Bible passage for her husband was from Isaiah 30:15, "In quietness and in confidence shall be your strength." When she saw a friend whom she had known since high school at her husband's memorial service in Buffalo, Suzie said to her, "I was very blessed. He (Eric Jr.) was a very good and wonderful husband and father. He was kind and generous. I am extremely grateful."

When Suzie Hedstrom passed away, about four years after her husband, the family had memorial services in both Sarasota, Florida, and in Buffalo, New York—as they had for Eric Jr. A friend of Suzie's from her high school days said at that time, "She had such a sense of spirituality. She is now with her God. She was a patient, loving and kind person."

Photographs for Chapter Five

Eric Jr. in Army Air Force
during WWII (age twenty-two).

Suzie Hedstrom at the time of
her engagement (age nineteen).

Suzie Hedstrom's parents—Sherlock A. Herrick
Sr. and Eloise (Stockton) Herrick.

View of the lake on the Farm from Eric Jr. and
Suzie's house in East Aurora, New York.

Eric Jr. and Suzie with their three boys.

Eric Jr. with the family's dog, "Mark."

Eric Jr. in front of the birthplace of his great-grandfather in Old Stockholm, Sweden (at Baggensgaten 21 in the Block Perseus).

Eric Jr. and Suzie having lunch at the
Glenridge in Sarasota, Florida.

Epilogue

The Hedstrom burial plot in Forest Lawn Cemetery in Buffalo, New York (Lot 88, Section 8), where all five of the Hedstroms featured in this book are buried next to each other.

For unto whomsoever much is given,
of him shall by much required

LUKE: 12:48

Epilogue

The primary audience for this book is the various members of the Hedstrom family who are now living and who may not yet be born. A secondary audience is the various living friends of Eric Jr. and Suzie Hedstrom in Western New York and in Sarasota, Florida. This book may also be of some interest to a few others in the general public who are interested in Swedish emigration or family histories in the US. The author assumes that the potential audience is not large. However, his motivation was to preserve the true story of the five individuals who are featured and their families.

What can be learned from reading about these ancestors? They all had qualities and physical attributes with which they were born, as well as events that intruded into their lives unexpectedly, such as wars and medical shocks. Mary, the wife of Eric Sr., once said, "It isn't the hand of cards that you are dealt; it's how you play them that counts."

Eric Jr. was once asked by the author how he thought about the concept of success in life. He replied, "I feel that success ultimately is achieving a balance between being reasonably successful with your family and friends, reasonably successful with your career, and reasonably successful at giving back to your community."

Acknowledgments

T he idea for this book passed through several iterations. First, the author's mother, Suzie Hedstrom, had an interest in genealogy as a hobby. After pursuing this hobby himself, the author found the nearly endless number of names and dates a bit uninteresting and looked to learn more of the story behind many of the individual ancestors. Then, having spent a lifetime collecting a great deal of information about the various forebears, the author realized what happens for so many people: the next generation is not sure who is in the photographs or what the context for all the various papers, so many of the items collected by one generation get thrown out by the next generation. By publishing this book, the author hopes to preserve as much of the full life story of the five individuals featured in these biographical sketches as possible.

The Douglas family contributed enormously to this project. Eric A. Douglas (1895–1953), grandson of Leonard Hedstrom, had possession of Erik J. Hedstrom's original diary and used it to write *The Hedstrom Story*, which proved to be a very helpful starting point for much of the family research. His son, William A. Douglas, corresponded with the author and provided additional helpful information as well as photos. His daughter, Mary (Douglas) Dick—a third cousin of the author—shared the original diary of Erik J. Hedstrom so that it could be photocopied.

Brenda (Hedstrom) Williams, sister of Eric Sr., and her husband, Harvey Williams, paid for very helpful research by Mr. Pontus Möller, the editor of the Swedish Peerage book and Riddarhusgenealog—chief of the Genealogical Department of Sweden's House of Nobility. They also had quite a bit of helpful correspondence related to Eric Sr, and the Cooper Paper Box Company.

Four individuals in Umea, Sweden, helped to locate the farmhouse of Jonas Hedstrom: Niklas Akerlund, librarian, Archives and Special Collections, Umea University Library, located Jonas Hedstrom's family "on the parish books of Umea landsforsamling." Mikael Björkman, a genealogist with the Sodravbforskare in Umea, found a 1788 map called the "Storskifte pa inagor" that showed Jonas Hedstrom's twelve parcels of land and the location of his farmhouse. Mikael's colleague, Tommy Jacobsson, calculated the total square meters of Jonas's twelve parcels of land (4,518.25) that translates into 1.12 acres.

Cilla Ingvarsson, collection registrar at Sweden's Maritime Museum & Aquarium in Gothenburg, found a painting of a Swedish sailing ship called the *Hindoo*, but we had no way of knowing whether it was the same ship that Erik, Charlotte, and Leonard took to immigrate to the US, so we did not end up including it.

Susanne Titus, head of library services at the Swenson Swedish Immigration Research Center in Rock Island,

Illinois, checked in all of that library's archives but was unable to find anything related to this Hedstrom family.

Finally, the author is deeply appreciative for the continuing love and support of his wife.

Select Bibliography

Books

Barton, Hildor Arnold. *A Folk Divided: Homeland Swedes and Swedish Americans, 1840–1940*. Carbondale: Southern Illinois Univ. Press, 1994.

Barton, H. Arnold. *Letters from the Promised Land: Swedes in America, 1840–1914*. Minneapolis: University of Minnesota Press for the Swedish Pioneer Historical Society, 2012.

Barton, Hildor Arnold. *Scandinavia in the Revolutionary Era, 1760–1815*. Minneapolis, MN: Univ. of Minn. Pr., 1986.

Benson, Adolph B., and Hedin, Nabolth. *Swedes in America, 1638–1938*. New Haven: Yale University Press, 1938.

Hedstrom, Arthur E. *Call Me Sonja*. Bloomington, IN: 2012.

Knox, Seymour H. *Polo Tales and Other Tales, 1921–1971.* Buffalo, New York: privately published, 1972.

Lyman, Frank H. *The City of Kenosha and Kenosha County, Wisconsin: a Record of Settlement, Organization, Progress, and Achievement. Volume I.* Tucson, AZ: W.C. & Cox Co., 1974. US Census, Lake County, IL, 1850.

Williams, Brenda Hedstrom, and Mitchell Warren Hedstrom. *Eric Jonsson Hedstrom: His Ancestors, Emigration, and Descendants, 1470–1977.* W.S. Sullwold Pub., 1978.

Yale University Class Book, Class of 1921, Biographies. "Eric Leonard Hedstrom." Also, Class Book of 1946 (Quarter Century Chronicle).

Articles

Betts, Paul. "Riviera resort shows off its Cannes-do attitude." *Financial Times* (Nov. 3, 2011).

Brown, Patricia Leigh. "Some in Reno Say Do Not Put Asunder Artifacts of Divorce." Refers to a 1931 law that allowed a person to obtain a divorce after they resided in the state for six weeks.

Brooke, James. "Okinawa Suicides and Japan's Army: Burying the Truth." *New York Times.* June 20, 2005.

Economist magazine. "Horse Play." (April 10, 1993).

Frost, Harlan M. "The Buffalo Federation of Churches—Beginnings." Niagara Frontier, Buffalo and Erie County Historical Society. Summer 1972. 41.

Hedstrom, Anna Clampffer. Obituary. *Buffalo Evening News*. May 3, 1929. 48.

Hedstrom, Anna Clampffer. Obituary. *Our Record*. June 1929.

Hedstrom, Eric L. "Doubles Position Play and Strategy—Part I." *American Lawn Tennis* (June 20,1937) and part II of the same article (August 5, 1937).

Hedstrom, Eric L. "More Emphasis on Shot Making—Part I." The Racquet. May 1952; and Part II of the same article. June 1952.

Hedstrom, Erik J. *Letter from a Swedish Emigrant in North America*, September 20, 1843, Aftonbladet Newspaper.

Hedstrom, Erik J. *An Emigrant Letter from 1843*. Published in The Swedish Pioneer Historical Quarterly. October 1981.

Hedstrom, Eric L. Obituary. 'Our Record', November 1894.

Hedstrom, Eric L Jr. Obituary. The Buffalo News. June 17, 2014.

Hedstrom, Katherine—"Mrs. Hedstrom Dies at 76; Girl Scout Booster." Buffalo Courier Express. June 27, 1952

Herrick, Eloise G.—"Miss Eloise G. Herrick Engaged. Buffalo Courier Express. September 11, 1949.

Herrick, Eloise G.—Obituary. Buffalo News. May 9, 2018.

History of Buffalo—Coal and Oil. 773–775

Mansfield, J. B., Editor. *History of the Great Lakes—Volume II.* Halton Hills, Ontario, Canada. 2003

Matthews, George E. *Men of New York—Volume II.* Buffalo, New York. 1898. 12D

Oldrin, John. "Tokeneke—A History." Reprinted from "Darien, 1641- 1820 1970—Historical

Sketches" with the permission of the Darien Historical Society.

Sylan, R. I., "Leader Militant." Town Tidings. July 1931. 36–37

Warren, Frank D. "Frank D. Warren Dies 66th Year", probably newspaper in Plainfield, New Jersey.

Watson, Bob. "Spalding-Yates: A Century of Keeping Buffalo Warm." Buffalo Evening News/April 10, 1959.

Young, Charley. "WNY Ruled Polo World." Buffalo Evening News. Date unknown. G-6. Refers to Arthur E. Hedstrom as being a two-goal polo player.

Unpublished Works

Bartolain, Paul L. Letter to the author dated December 14, 1983; Vice President, Chicago Title Insurance Company; 15 South County Street; Waukegan, IL

60085; Hedstrom, Bonnie (Mrs. Lars Hedstrom Jr.). *Hedstrom and Pohorilak Families, Their Related Ancestors and Descendants.* July 13, 2012 'Current working copy'.

Hedstrom, Eric Leonard Sr.—War Service Certificate (No. 413373). United States Navy.

Hedstrom, Eric Leonard Sr.—Curriculum Vitae

Hedstrom, Eric Leonard Jr.—"The Story of Cooper Paper Box." May 16, 1961

Hedstrom, Eric Leonard Jr. Chronology of My Life

Hedstrom, Erik J. *Diary.* November 3, 1860 and updated by him before he died.

Hedstrom, Mary (Warren). Chronology of My Life

Hedstrom, Mitchell W. "Miscellaneous Notes—Taken from Visits with Gran."

Surrogate's Court, Erie County, New York. "Transfer Tax— In the matter of the Estate of Anna M. Hedstrom. May 2, 1929.

Websites

Delaware Avenue Baptist Church—Website for history of church: https://buffaloah.com/how/2/2.10/delave.html

Notes

The names of Hedstrom family members are abbreviated as follows in the notes:

EJH	Erik Jonsson Hedstrom ("Erik")
ELH	Eric Leonard Hedstrom ("Leonard")
AEH	Arthur Eric Hedstrom ("Arthur")
ELH Sr.	Eric Leonard Hedstrom Sr. ("Eric Sr.")
ELH Jr.	Eric Leonard Hedstrom Jr. ("Eric Jr.")

Author's Note Regarding Names

1 Williams, *Eric Jonsson Hedstrom*, 30, 33 for birth records.
2 Williams, *Eric Jonsson Hedstrom*, 62 for Erik's name in his letter to Pehr.

Introduction

1 Williams, *Eric Jonsson Hedstrom*, 127 for reference to Eric Stolterman, his wife, and their three children. In Sweden in those years, it was common for men to adopt a different surname.

For example, Jonas Hedstrom's father, Eric Stolterman, took his surname since his father was named Eric Olofsson.

2   Williams, *Eric Jonsson Hedstrom,* xii.

3   The author counted the names during a trip to Stockholm in 1971.

Chapter 1—Erik Jonsson Hedstrom

1   EJH *Diary.*

2   Williams, *Eric Jonsson Hedstrom*, 30, 33.

3   Williams, *Eric Jonsson Hedstrom*, 30,

4   EJH *Diary,*

5   Map is included at the end of chapter 1 Explanation of how map was found is in the acknowledgments section.

6   Williams, *Eric Jonsson Hedstrom*, 127, 128.

7   Wikipedia for "Napoleonic Wars," "Treaties of Tilset," and "Finnish War."

8   Barton, Hildor Arnold. *Scandinavia*, 292.

9   Barton, Hildor Arnold. *A Folk Divided*, 7, 8.

10 Wikipedia for "Finnish Famine of 1866–1868" and "Swedish Famine of 1867–1869."

11 Wikipedia for "Penicillin."

12 Discussions the author and his daughter had with people in Umea.

13 Williams, *Eric Jonsson Hedstrom*, 17–47 and 125–128.

14 EJH *Diary.*

15 Williams, *Eric Jonsson Hedstrom*, 17.

16 EJH *Diary.*

17 Williams, *Eric Jonsson Hedstrom*, 138.

18 EJH *Diary.*

19 EJH *Diary.*

20 Williams, *Eric Jonsson Hedstrom*, 139.

21 Williams, *Eric Jonsson Hedstrom*, 139.

22 Williams, *Eric Jonsson Hedstrom*, 128.

23 EJH *Diary.*

24 The address where the son, Eric Leonard Hedstrom, was born ("Baggensgatan 21 in the block Perseus") is the third residence where Erik lived in Old Stockholm, which can be seen today. For visitors to Old Stockholm, the entire town is easy to walk around. The five residences where Erik lived were as follows:

- *Block Pyramus, house #6 near Stora Nygatan.* Erik lived here in 1825 when he was a journeyman. The house is no longer there.
- *Sven Vintappares grand 3 (or 6) in the block called Alcmene*—"Sven the vintner's alley." Erik lived here before he was married. His mother, then referred to as "the widow Boberg," was "his housekeeper." He probably had his workshop on the bottom floor facing the yard. Erik lived here in 1833–1834.
- *Baggensgatan 21 in the block Perseus.* This is where Erik was living with his wife, Charlotte, when their son, Eric Leonard, was born. The photo of Eric L. Hedstrom Jr. (and also the photo of the author and his daughter on the back cover) in this book was taken in front of the door to this house.
- *Kindstugatan No. 5, near Kopmantorget.* Erik, Charlotte, and Leonard lived here from 1835 to 1842—quite a long time.
- *Kopmangatan No. 9, near Kopmangatan* (Merchant Street) *and Stortorget* (Big Market). Erik and his family lived here shortly before departing for America.

As a footnote, Erik's brother Pehr lived in a very nice house nearly opposite the Storkyrkan (Big Church). His house was at Trangsund 10.

25 EJH *Diary.*

26 Hildor Arnold Barton, *A Folk Divided*, xiii.

27 Hildor Arnold Barton, *A Folk Divided*, xii, 3, 4, 8, 9.

28 Adolph B. Benson and Nabolth Hedin, *Swedes in America*, 79.

29 Hildor Arnold Barton, *A Folk Divided*, 15, and Wikipedia for "Church of Sweden."

30 Adolph B. Benson and Nabolth Hedin, *Swedes in America*, 81, 82.

31 Hildor Arnold Barton, *A Folk Divided*, 3, 5.

32 Hildor Arnold Barton, *A Folk Divided*, 14.

33 Wikipedia for "General Land Office."

34 Wikipedia for "Preemption Act of 1841," "Homestead Act of 1862," and "Manifest Destiny."

35 Adolph B. Benson and Nabolth Hedin, Nabolth. *Swedes in America*, 80.

36 Adolph B. Benson and Nabolth Hedin, Nabolth. *Swedes in America*, 78, and Hildor Arnold Barton, *A Folk Divided*, 13, 14.

37 Adolph B. Benson and Nabolth Hedin, *Swedes in America*, 78, 81, and Hildor Arnold Barton, *A Folk Divided*, 14, 17.

38 Adolph B. Benson and Nabolth Hedin, *Swedes in America*, 78, 79, 187.

39 Adolph B. Benson and Nabolth Hedin, *Swedes in America*, 81, 82.

40 Wikipedia for "Demographics of Sweden" and "US Population 1800."

41 Adolph B. Benson and Nabolth Hedin, *Swedes in America*, 79, 80, 82.

42 Wikipedia for "Ellis Island" and "Erie Canal."

43 Frank H. Lyman, *The City of Kenosha*, 132.

44 EJH *Diary.*

45 US Census, Lake County, IL, 1850. This census shows the family group with Eric Headstram as the husband, age forty-seven, who was born in Sweden and who had the occupation of farmer. It shows Charlotte as his wife, age forty-five, also born in Sweden. And it shows Leonard as the son, age fifteen, also born in Sweden, listed as farmer and attended school in Newport.

46 Paul L. Bartolain, letter to the author.

47 Wikipedia for "Louisiana Purchase," "Illinois became state," "Wisconsin became state," and "Lincoln-Douglas Debates."

48 Erik J. Hedstrom, *An Emigrant Letter,* 241.

49 EJH *Diary.*

50 Williams, *Eric Jonsson Hedstrom*, 98, and Bonnie Hedstrom (Mrs. Lars Hedstrom Jr.), *Hedstrom and Pohorilak Families,* 9.
51 EJH *Diary.*
52 Bonnie Hedstrom, *Hedstrom and Pohorilak Families,* 9.
53 EJH *Diary.*
54 Williams, *Eric Jonsson Hedstrom*, 98.
55 Williams, *Eric Jonsson Hedstrom*, 75.
56 Williams, *Eric Jonsson Hedstrom*, 66.
57 Williams, *Eric Jonsson Hedstrom*, 75.
58 EJH *Diary.*
59 Erik J. Hedstrom, *An Emigrant Letter.*

Chapter 2—Eric Leonard Hedstrom

1 The Hedstrom family had the dissolution notice for the Meeker-Hedstrom business that was dated June 26, 1885.
2 Williams, *Eric Jonsson Hedstrom*, 67.
3 Williams, *Eric Jonsson Hedstrom*, 129, 139.
4 EJH *Diary.*
5 Bonnie Hedstrom, *Hedstrom and Pohorilak Families,* 9.
6 Williams, *Eric Jonsson Hedstrom*, 71–73.
7 Bonnie Hedstrom, *Hedstrom and Pohorilak Families,* 13, 14.
8 Williams, *Eric Jonsson Hedstrom*, 66.
9 Williams, *Eric Jonsson Hedstrom*, 66, 67.
10 J. B. Mansfield, editor, *History of the Great Lakes;* George E. Matthews, *Men of New York and History of Buffalo—Coal and Oil.*
11 J. B. Mansfield, editor, *History of the Great Lakes,* 12D.
12 Website for Delaware Avenue Baptist Church.
13 Williams, *Eric Jonsson Hedstrom*, 89, and Eric L. Hedstrom, obituary. *Our Record.*
14 Williams, *Eric Jonsson Hedstrom*, 75.
15 Bonnie Hedstrom, *Hedstrom and Pohorilak Families,* 12.
16 The Hedstrom family has copies of Leonard's tickets for the Palace that day.
17 Williams, *Eric Jonsson Hedstrom*, 68.

18 Williams, *Eric Jonsson Hedstrom*, 88.

19 Anna Clampffer Hedstrom, obituary, *Buffalo Evening News,* and Anna Clampffer Hedstrom, obituary, *Our Record.*

Chapter 3—Arthur Eric Hedstrom

1   Williams, *Eric Jonsson Hedstrom*, 83.

2   Williams, *Eric Jonsson Hedstrom*, 82.

3   Paul Betts, "Riviera resort shows off …" In the 1860s, Britain's Lord Chancellor, Henry Brougham, "discovered" Cannes and helped to turn it into an exclusive winter resort for the old British aristocracy. Since 1946, the annual Film Festival has attracted many tourists. However, in more recent times, the town is popular among French and European retirees, with the peak season being more like May to October instead of February and March.

4   The manuscript for *Call Me Sonja* was handed down from Arthur Hedstrom to his daughter, Brenda. It was in the form of a pile of typed pages in a white box with a pink bow around it. Brenda kept the manuscript in her attic and had completely forgotten about it until the author discovered it when he was helping Brenda clean out her attic one day. She gave it to the author, who didn't have time to read it until many years later. While reading it for the first time, the author quickly realized that it was an unusually good story and arranged to have it published.

5   Williams, *Eric Jonsson Hedstrom*, 75.

6   Williams, *Eric Jonsson Hedstrom*, 76.

7   Williams, *Eric Jonsson Hedstrom*, 76.

8   Williams, *Eric Jonsson Hedstrom*, 68.

9   Williams, *Eric Jonsson Hedstrom*, 68.

10 Williams, *Eric Jonsson Hedstrom*, 77, 78.

11 Williams, *Eric Jonsson Hedstrom*, 76.

12 Williams, *Eric Jonsson Hedstrom*, 78.

13 Hedstrom, Katherine—"Mrs. Hedstrom Dies …"

14 Williams, *Eric Jonsson Hedstrom*, 81.

15 Wikipedia for "Popocatepetl." The author notes that "this is very much an active volcano." The Wikipedia article notes that this volcanic mountain erupted nine times during 2019.

16 Family records.

17 Williams, *Eric Jonsson Hedstrom*, 81.

18 The reference to Arthur serving on the Mexican border with Troop One in WWI raises the question of how Mexico got involved in WWI. According to Wikipedia for "Mexico in World War 1," during this time, although Mexico was a neutral country in WWI, it was embroiled in a full-scale civil war that was eventually settled in 1915. However, Germany had made several attempts to incite war between Mexico and the US to draw America into a battle on its southern border and prevent it from assisting Britain and France in their battle against Germany.

19 Williams, *Eric Jonsson Hedstrom*, 89.

20 Williams, *Eric Jonsson Hedstrom*, 80.

21 Williams, *Eric Jonsson Hedstrom*, 109, 120.

22 The list of coal trestles and coal yards was found on a piece of stationery for the E. L. Hedstrom—Buffalo Coal Company.

23 Bob Watson, "Spalding-Yates …"

24 Williams, *Eric Jonsson Hedstrom*, 89.

25 Family records show that the Cooper Paper Box Company was a similar size as the E. L. Hedstrom Coal Company. The former had annual revenues of approximately $1 million for their fiscal year ended December 31, 1957, and the latter had annual revenues of $1.4 million for their fiscal year ended January 31, 1948.

26 Harlan M. Frost, "The Buffalo Federation of Churches …"

27 Williams, *Eric Jonsson Hedstrom*, 89.

28 R. I. Sylan, "Leader Militant."

29 Surrogate's Court, Erie County.

30 Williams, *Eric Jonsson Hedstrom*, 88.

31 Williams, *Eric Jonsson Hedstrom*, 82.

32 Williams, *Eric Jonsson Hedstrom*, 93–95.

33 Williams, *Eric Jonsson Hedstrom*, 67.

34 Katherine Hedstrom—"Mrs. Hedstrom Dies …"

35 In stating that "he managed to grow the nest egg," the author compared the amount of his inheritance with the amount of his estate when he died, adjusting both figures using the US Bureau of Labor Statistics' "CPI Inflation Calculator" to convert them to 2019 dollars.

36 Williams, *Eric Jonsson Hedstrom*, 118.

37 Williams, *Eric Jonsson Hedstrom*, 118.

Chapter 4—Eric L. Hedstrom Sr.

1 "Eric L. Hedstrom Weds Miss Warren" and "Mary Warren a Bride"—two articles from newspapers for which we do not have the names of the newspapers or the dates. We assume one was the Plainfield, New Jersey, newspaper and the other was a Buffalo, New York, newspaper.

2 Mary (Warren) Hedstrom, Chronology.

3 Mary (Warren) Hedstrom, Chronology.

4 Frank D. Warren, "Frank D. Warren Dies," and Mary (Warren) Hedstrom, Chronology.

5 Mary (Warren) Hedstrom, Chronology.

6 The typed letter from President Taft was dated July 6, 1916. It was on his stationery that had "William H. Taft; New Haven, Conn." at the top, although just above the date, it had Pointe-au-Pic, Canada." The letter was addressed to Frank D. Warren at 966 Hillside Avenue in Plainfield, New Jersey. It read, "I have your very kind note of June 25th and thank you for sending the umbrella. I had no right to impose the burden on you, but men are sometimes forgetful—women never. Please present my very respectful compliments and the regards of a kinsman to Mrs. Warren. Sincerely yours."

7 Eric Leonard Hedstrom Sr.—curriculum vitae.

8 Yale University Class Book and Eric Leonard Hedstrom Sr.—curriculum vitae.

9 Wikipedia for "World War I End."

10 Eric Leonard Hedstrom Sr.—curriculum vitae. On the topic of golf, Eric Jr. once said that Arthur Hedstrom would usually shoot in the seventies or low eighties and that his father, Eric Sr., would usually shoot in the eighties. He (Eric Jr.) usually shot in the low nineties.

11 Mary (Warren) Hedstrom, Chronology.

12 Family papers include the letter from Frank D. Warren to his son describing the visit he and his wife had at Four Winds Farm in Buffalo, New York.

13 Mary (Warren) Hedstrom, Chronology.

14 Mary (Warren) Hedstrom, Chronology.

15 Mary (Warren) Hedstrom, Chronology.

16 *Economist* magazine, "Horse Play."

17 Eric L. Hedstrom, "Doubles Position Play …" and Eric L. Hedstrom, "More Emphasis on Shot Making …"

18 Family notes.

19 Eric Leonard Hedstrom Sr.—curriculum vitae.

20 Eric Leonard Hedstrom Sr.—curriculum vitae.

21 Mary (Warren) Hedstrom, Chronology.

22 Mary (Warren) Hedstrom, Chronology .

23 Patricia Leigh Brown, "Some in Reno."

24 Mary (Warren) Hedstrom, Chronology.

25 Family notes.

26 Mary (Warren) Hedstrom, Chronology.

27 Mary (Warren) Hedstrom, Chronology.

28 Mary (Warren) Hedstrom, Chronology.

29 Mary (Warren) Hedstrom, Chronology.

30 Eric Leonard Hedstrom Jr., Chronology.

31 Eric Leonard Hedstrom Jr., Chronology.

32 Eric Leonard Hedstrom Jr., Chronology.

33 Eric Leonard Hedstrom Jr., Chronology.

34 Eric Leonard Hedstrom Jr., Chronology.

35 Eric Leonard Hedstrom Jr., Chronology.

36 Eric Leonard Hedstrom Jr., Chronology.

37 Eric Leonard Hedstrom Jr., Chronology.

38 Eric Leonard Hedstrom Jr., Chronology.

39 Family notes.

40 Wikipedia for "Cecil Elaine Eustace Smith (figure skater)," Eric Sr.'s second wife.

41 Family notes.

42 Family notes.

43 Board minutes of Cooper Paper Box Company, January 20, 1956.

44 Darien Historical?

45 Eric Sr. and Ethel (Hoyt) Peale were introduced to each other by Preston ("Prep") Porter, who had married Carl Cooke's sister.

46 Eric Leonard Hedstrom Jr., Chronology.

Chapter 5—Eric L. Hedstrom Jr.

1 Publicly available materials and press releases from Graphic Controls.

2 Eric L. Hedstrom Jr., obituary.

3 Eric Leonard Hedstrom Jr., Chronology.

4 Eric Leonard Hedstrom Jr., Chronology.

5 Eric Leonard Hedstrom Jr., Chronology.

6 Eric Leonard Hedstrom Jr., Chronology.

7 Eric Leonard Hedstrom Jr., Chronology.

8 Eric Leonard Hedstrom Jr., US Army discharge papers.

9 James Brooke, "Okinawa Suicides …"

10 Eric Leonard Hedstrom Jr., Chronology.

11 Eric Leonard Hedstrom Jr., Chronology.

12 Letter from Eric L. Hedstrom Jr. to his mother, dated June 1949.

13 Eloise G. Herrick—"Miss Eloise G. Herrick …"

14 Eric Leonard Hedstrom Jr., Chronology.

15 Family notes.

16 Family notes.

17 Eric Leonard Hedstrom Jr., Chronology.

18 Eric Leonard Hedstrom Jr., Chronology.

19 Eric Leonard Hedstrom Jr., Chronology.

20 Eric Leonard Hedstrom Jr., Chronology.

21 Eric Leonard Hedstrom Jr., Chronology.

22 Eric Leonard Hedstrom Jr., Chronology.

23 Eric Leonard Hedstrom Jr., Chronology.

24 Eric Leonard Hedstrom Jr., Chronology.

25 Graphic Controls Corporation financial statements.

26 Letter from Eric L. Hedstrom Jr. to family members in early 1959.

27 Eric Leonard Hedstrom Jr., Chronology.

28 Eric Leonard Hedstrom Jr., Chronology.

29 Eric Leonard Hedstrom Jr., Chronology.

30 Eric Leonard Hedstrom Jr., Chronology.

31 Eric Leonard Hedstrom Jr., Chronology.

32 Eric Leonard Hedstrom Jr., Chronology.

33 Eric L Hedstrom Jr., obituary.

34 Eloise G. Herrick, obituary.